SEIN 2010
University of Plymouth, Plymouth, UK
24-28 November 2010

Proceedings of the Sixth Collaborative Research Symposium on Security, E-learning, Internet and Networking

Editors
Paul S Dowland
Bernhard G Humm
Martin H Knahl

Centre for Security, Communications and Network Research
University of Plymouth

ISBN: 978-1-84102-269-7

© 2010 Centre for Security, Communications and Network Research,
University of Plymouth, Plymouth, UK
All rights reserved

No part of this book may be reproduced, stored in a retrieval system, or transmitted in any form or by any means – electronic, mechanical, photocopy, recording or otherwise, without the prior written permission of the publisher or distributor.

Preface

This book presents the Proceedings of the Sixth Collaborative Research Symposium on Security, E-learning, Internet and Networking, hosted by the University of Plymouth, Plymouth, UK, on the 24-28th November 2010.

There have already been five former Research Symposia in June 2005, October 2006, June 2007 and November 2008/2009, hosted by the University of Applied Sciences Darmstadt, Germany; Glyndŵr University, UK and the University of Plymouth, UK.

We have chosen the name SEIN reflecting the first letters of our joint areas of research:

- Security
- E-learning
- Internet and applications
- Networking

All authors are researchers from the University of Plymouth, University of Applied Sciences Darmstadt, and Furtwangen University of Applied Sciences, Germany. They are all PhD students or postdoctoral researchers working in the presented areas. We hope this book can show new and interesting ideas for a wide audience especially for those who could not attend the Symposium.

Paul S Dowland
Steven M Furnell
Vic Grout
Bernhard G Humm
Martin H Knahl

Symposium Organisers
Plymouth, November 2010

About the CSCAN Network

The SEIN series of symposiums is organised by the CSCAN Network.

The Centre for Security, Communications and Network Research (CSCAN) is a specialised information technology and networking research facility at the University of Plymouth. Originally established in 1985, CSCAN conducts research in the areas of IT security, communications, Internet & WWW technologies and mobility. The centre has a proven pedigree, including projects conducted for, and in collaboration with, commercial companies, as well as participation in European research initiatives. Over the years, our research activities have led to numerous successful projects, along with associated publications and patents.

The CSCAN Network has been established to facilitate research co-operation with other academic institutions. The first node was established at the University of Applied Sciences, Darmstadt, Germany, with a number of participating academic staff and active research projects. The Centre for Applied Internet Research (CAIR) at Glyndŵr University joined in 2007 as an adjunct node. Most recently, the University of Applied Sciences, Furtwangen, Germany, was established as a further node in June 2010.

	Address	Centre for Security, Communications and Network Research University of Plymouth Drake Circus, Plymouth, PL4 8AA, UK
	Email	info@cscan.org
	URL	www.cscan.org

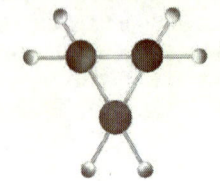

Address	aida - Institute of Applied Informatics Darmstadt University of Applied Sciences Darmstadt Haardtring 100, D-64295 Darmstadt, Germany
Email	aida@h-da.de
URL	www.aida.h-da.de

Address	Furtwangen University Faculty of Business Information Systems (WI) Robert-Gerwig-Platz 1, 78120 Furtwangen Germany
Email	wi-phd@hs-furtwangen.de
URL	www.hs-furtwangen.de/fachbereiche/wi

Address	Centre for Applied Internet Research (CAIR) Glyndŵr University Plas Coch Campus, Mold Road, Wrexham, LL11 2AW, UK
Email	contact@cair-uk.org
URL	www.cair-uk.org

Contents

Introducing a Framework and Methodological Guidance for Model Based Testing ... 1
M.George, K.P.Fischer-Hellmann, M.Knahl, U.Bleimann, and S.Atkinson

A New Architectural-Approach for Next Generation Automotive Applications ... 11
M.Glaab, W.Fuhrmann, J.Wietzke and B.V.Ghita

An Approach for Structuring Heterogeneous Automotive Software Systems by use of Multicore Architectures ... 19
A.Knirsch, J.Wietzke, R.Moore and P.S.Dowland

Towards a Classification of Information Technology Governance Frameworks ... 31
M.Krey, B.Harriehausen, M.Knoll and S.M.Furnell

Agile Limitations and Model-Driven Opportunities for Software Development Projects ... 43
K.Mairon, M.Buchheit, M.Knahl, S.Atkinson, S.M.Furnell and U.Schreier

System Design for Embedded Automotive Systems ... 53
S.Vergata, J.Wietzke, A.Schütte and P.S.Dowland

Integration of Model-Based Functional Testing Procedures within a Creation Environment for Value Added Services ... 61
P.Wacht, A.Lehmann, T.Eichelmann, W.Fuhrmann, U.Trick and B.V.Ghita

Author Index ... 75

Introducing a Framework and Methodological Guidance for Model Based Testing

M.George[1,4], K.P.Fischer-Hellmann[1,2], M.Knahl[3], U.Bleimann[1] and S.Atkinson[4]

[1]Aida Institute of Applied Informatics Darmstadt, Darmstadt, Germany
[2]Digamma Communications Consulting GmbH, Mühltal, Germany
[3]Furtwangen University of Applied Sciences, Furtwangen, Germany
[4]Centre for Security, Communications, and Network Research,
University of Plymouth, Plymouth, United Kingdom
e-mail:george.mathew@hotmail.com

Abstract

The growing complexities of software and the demand for shorter time-to-market are two important challenges that face today's IT industry. These challenges demand the increase of both productivity and quality of software. Early integration of test development into the system life cycle becomes more and more important, which helps the developer to find the errors in an early stage of design and development. A promising technique for the early integration of test development in system life cycle is model based testing that automatically generates test artefacts from design models. A major challenge of model based testing is the lack of methodological guidance, approaches, and a framework. My research aims to define a methodological guidance and a framework that facilitates model based testing which ranges from requirement specification, modelling guide lines, test generation from models, test management, and traceability of requirements to models and generated tests. In this paper, we define and justify the research problem and present a research approach.

Keywords

Model based testing, UML, Model, Test oracles, Traceability

1. Introduction

Today's software testing methodologies and techniques have to meet the growing complexities of the software and shorter time-to-market. Testing is an essential activity in software engineering. In the simplest terms, it amounts to observing the execution of a software system to validate whether it behaves as intended and identify potential malfunctions (Bertolino, 2007). Today's software testing ranges from unit test to software acceptance tests, but all these tests are confined in the later stages of development. Major problem of this approach is that testing is not done at the early stages of development and defects in the design and specification detected in the later stages of software development process are expensive to fix.

Automation of software development and software testing on the basis of executable models and simulation promises significant reductions in fault-removal cost and development time. (Utting et al. 2006) defines Model based testing as a variant of testing that relies on explicit behaviour models that encode the intended behaviour of a system and possibly the behaviour of its environment. According to Bertolino (Bertolino, 2007), the major goal of model based testing (MBT) is automatic generation of test artefacts from models. Model Based Testing offers considerable promise in reducing the cost of test generation, increasing the effectiveness of the tests, and shortening the testing effort. (Dalal et al. 1999)

While using the model based testing in practical software life cycle, the main problem arise is the lack of a methodological guidance and a process for defining the requirements, developing models, generating tests, tracing requirements to models and the test cases generated from models, test selection criteria (example, transition coverage) and test management(defining priorities and number of execution of each tests, defining priorities of requirements, "etc..") that suites for model based testing. Our research will focus to develop and define a framework for the above.

This paper is organized into an overview of Model Based Testing, its challenges, problem description of the research work, problem justification and an overview of the research approach.

2. Model Based Testing and Challenges

Fundamental approach of Model Based Testing is to effectively use models defined in software development to drive the testing process, in particular to automatically generate test cases and test suite and enable the tests at the early stages of development. There are different definitions for Model Based Testing. Mark Utting (Utting et al. 2006) defines it as the "generation of test cases with test oracles from behavioural model". Since Models describes the behaviour of the system, tests can be executed based on the model for quality software. Bertolino refers it as the test case derivation from a model representing software behaviour. (Bertolino et al 2005)

Model-based testing typically involves the following steps: (Utting et al. 2007, Legeard, 2010)

- Building an abstract model of the behaviour of the system under test. The model captures a subset of the system requirements.
- Definition of test selection criteria. The criteria define what test cases to be generated from the model.
- Generating abstract tests from the model, using the defined test selection criteria. At this stage, the generated test cases are expressed in terms of the abstractions used by the model.
- Transforming (concretize) the abstract test cases into executable test cases.
- Executing the test cases. At execution time, an adaptor component transforms the output of the system to the abstraction of the model.
- Assigning of a pass/fail verdict to executed test case.
- Analyzing the execution result.

Model based testing significantly reduces testing time (Bringmann et al. 2008). According to Legard (Legeard, 2010), Model Based Testing is an important and useful technique that brings significant progress over the state of the practice for functional software testing effectiveness, increasing productivity, and improving functional coverage. Following section describes various challenges of model based testing.

2.1. Modelling

A great deal of research focuses on automatic test generation from models Since Model Driven Development is emerging as the de-facto standard in software development (Frankel, 2003), research has to focus on building ideal models for quality software. (Bertolino, 2007).

Bertolino outlines "Test Based Modelling" as a dream in the software testing process. Instead of taking a model and see how well it is exploited for testing, it is better to consider how one should ideally build a model so that the software can be effectively tested (Bertolino, 2007). Today's software industry demands time to market and a high quality for the delivered software. This demands a growing need of research in Model Based testing as well with an extra focus in building models. Since models serve as the back bone of Model Based Testing, we have to develop concepts and methodologies that guide the model development.

2.2. Test Oracles in Model Based Testing

The functionality of the system is tested by comparing the output of the system for a predefined input, using a test oracle. The purpose of the test oracle is to give a test verdict ("Pass", "Fail", "Inconclusive", "etc."). A test oracle is a mechanism that determines the expected output for a given input and compares it with the actual output. The precision and efficiency of oracles greatly affects testing cost/effectiveness. Efficient test oracles are also a major factor for efficient test automation. An important component of testing is the oracle. Indeed, a test is meaningful only if it is possible to decide about its outcome (Bertolino, 2003). So an approach is needed for realizing and automating test oracles from models, an approach to generate test oracles automatically from models and requirements. Generated test oracles will be later used in the test execution phase to determine whether the test has passed or failed.

2.3. Traceability of Requirements in Model Based Testing

The automation of bidirectional traceability between requirements and test cases is a key aspect of MBT (Legeard, 2010). Bidirectional traceability is the ability to trace links between two parts of the software development process with respect to each other (Legeard, 2010). Dalal et al. suggests that defects of a model can be minimized by ensuring the traceability from requirements to the part of models (Dalal et al. 1999). Traceability of requirements is an integral part of Model Based Testing and provides effective verification to determine the coverage of requirements with respect to a model or models. Study has to be focused on how traceability of requirements can be propagated from system model and the tests generated from the model. That means the study has to be focussed on how system specification can be formulated and how system models can be developed for automatic test generation that helps to trace the requirements.

2.4. Automatic Test Generation and Evaluation

Fundamental approach and the effectiveness of model based testing is the automation that it offers (Bertolino, 2007) .Test suites and test cases are generated algorithmically from models and an execution framework executes the generated tests. The results are evaluated with respect to the expected outputs. Test cases can be generated using different techniques and can be executed in different target languages or execution frameworks such as TTCN3 or JUnit Tests. Here the TTCN3 & JUnit are only considered as a framework for executing the tests generated from models. Tests generated from models could be tests defined using TTCN3, or using some other high level languages or scripting languages. Bertolino views 100% automation (test generation and evaluation of test results) as a challenge in model based testing (Bertolino, 2007). These all demands an additional focus in 100% automation in model based testing, which can only be achieved by efficient test generation techniques.

3. Problem Description

Using models in testing demands a high quality modelling; otherwise the tests generated will not meet the intended goals. Correctness of a model is fundamental necessity to start the test case generation process. If the model is wrong, the generated tests will be invalid.(Dias Neto et al. 2007). Requirements specification also plays a major role in effective and efficient Model Based Testing. Zave classifies the goals of requirements engineering in her article. 'Understanding the priorities of the system', 'obtaining specifications that are well-suited for design and implementation activities' are two among them (Zave, 1997). Requirements specified by the business analyst can be annotated by the Test analyst. Requirement specification in the MBT process should define the test priority of each requirement, test selection criteria, model dependency, "etc.". In model based testing literature several test selection criteria and test generation algorithm can be found as shown in several surveys like [9] or [10]. Most of these algorithms generate thousands of tests (Test case explosion) and several tests generated are difficult to interpret and unambiguous. Also the tests generated need not be executed each and every time. There should be a mechanism for defining a test management process and requirements specification that provides the effective test generation and test execution. Traceability is another issue in model based testing, tests generated from models without tracing them to requirements cannot minimise the defects in models and it will be difficult to analyse the test results. (Dalal et al. 1999)

The problems mentioned above demand a framework /methodological guidance for defining a process that defines requirement specification, modelling, test management, test generation that is well suited for Model Based Testing. Table 1 summarises the research problem and criteria.

Problem	Criteria
Modelling	Model structure, Test Oracles
Requirement specification	Traceability, Requirements priority, Model dependency, Test Oracles
Test Generation	Test generation algorithm
Test Management/Test Explosion	Test priority, Test Selection, Result Analysis

Table 1: List of research problems and appropriate criteria

4. Related Work

A great deal of research has been already done in the field of Model Based Testing especially in field of test generation from Models. Offutt and Abdurazik (Offut et al 2000 and Offut et al. 1999) introduce methodologies for test generation from state-chart diagrams as well as from collaboration diagrams. The test generation is accomplished both using the static and dynamic models. This is considered to be the first approach in Model Based Testing (Dias Neto et al. 2007).

Mingsong use Unified Modelling Language (UML) activity diagrams as design specifications and present an automatic test case generation approach. The approach first randomly generates test cases for a JAVA program under test (Mingsong, 2006). Vieira et al. use UML use cases and activity diagrams to describe which functionalities should be tested and how to test them, respectively. This combination has the potential to create a very large number of test cases. The approach is demonstrated and evaluated based on use cases developed for testing a graphical user interface (GUI) (Vieira et al. 2006)

Soldal defines an algorithm for deriving tests from sequence diagram specifications that takes into consideration the partial nature of sequence diagrams as well as the notion of invalid and universal behaviour introduced in UML version 2.0 with the operators neg and assert (Soldal, 2006). Naslavsky proposes an approach that leverages model transformation traceability techniques to create fine-grained relationships among model-based testing artefacts (Naslavsky, 2006). Cavarra and Chrichton present a architecture for model-based testing using a profile of the UML. Class, object, and state diagrams are used to define essential models: descriptions that characterize the entire range of possible behaviours, in terms of the actions and events of the model. Object and state diagrams are used to introduce test directives (Cavarra et al. 2000).

Emanuela et al. suggest a procedure based on model-based testing techniques with test cases generated from UML sequence diagrams. The proposal is focused on mobile applications (Emanuela et al. 2007). Samuel et al. [19] have proposed automatic test case generation for UML state diagrams. It covers all the events associated with state diagrams (Samuel et al. 2008).

Prasanna and Chandran propose an approach for test generation from object diagrams using a "genetic tree crossover" algorithm. They present a banking system as a case study to justify this approach (Prasanna et al. 2009). Sarma et al. suggest test case generation from use case and sequence diagrams. These diagrams are converted to a "use case diagram graph" and a "sequence diagram graph" that are then used for test generation (Sarma et al. 2007).

There are also academic proposals available in the field of test generation using the UML & UML Testing Profile (U2TP). With the increasing complexity of Software Systems, effective tests are needed. UML does not provide the means of describing test. OMG (Object Management Group) has defined the profile of UML tests, called U2TP. U2TP fills the gap between designers and testers by providing the means to use UML in system modelling and tests specification [22]. Dai introduces a methodology on how to use the U2TP to transform a model of UML system design. He presents the definition of transformation rules from UML models to U2TP models (Dai, 2004). Zander et al. present an approach to automatically derive executable tests from UML diagrams using the UML Testing Profile (U2TP). The proposal presents a transformation from UML to executable tests (model to executable tests) using U2TP (Zander et al. 2005).

A close examination of the research work reveals the lack of a methodological guidance and an approach for the MBT. All the proposals described above provide one or several approaches for generating tests from models but do not attempt to provide a framework and guidelines for requirement specification, modelling, tests generation, test management, and traceability of requirements to models and tests that suites model based testing.

5. Research Approach

This section presents a research approach, early ideas for solving the above mentioned problems. The proposed solution is intended in the area of UML and business information systems and an evaluation of this approach will be accomplished by a case study. The solution proposed in this section is still at an early stage and only provides an overview and direction of the research approach. Figure 1, shows an overview of the proposed solution.Our research aims to propose a model-based testing framework, process, and methodology to cope with the above mentioned problem. At the current stage of the research, this framework is expected to incorporate the following steps: Figure 1 shows an overview of the proposed model based testing process and Figure 2 shows detailed approach of the proposed framework.

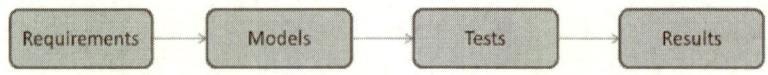

Figure 1: Model-based testing process, overview diagram

5.1. Requirement specification

In the first step, the business analyst specifies the requirements; framework/process defines all needed information such as requirement priority, dependency to other requirements and related model artefact that are important in a business analyst perspective. Afterwards, the test analyst will annotate the requirements with all needed information for test generation, such as test priority and test selection criteria. See "Requirement specification" in Figure 2.

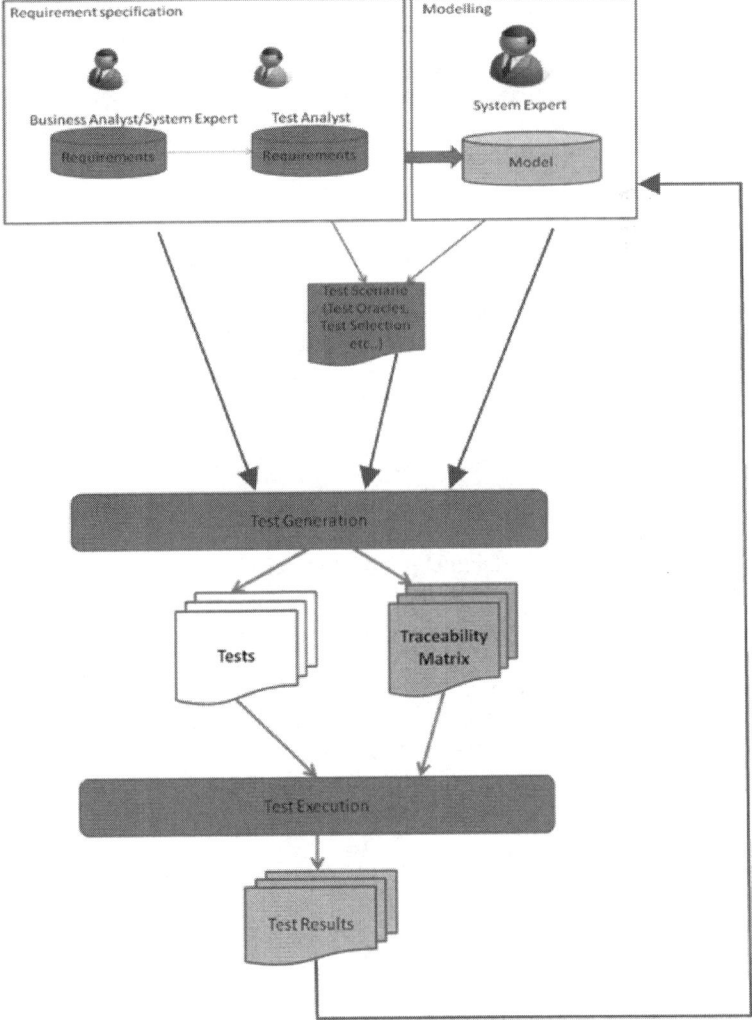

Figure 2: Model- based testing process, detailed diagram

5.2. Modelling

A design using UML will be described by the system expert. Additional information required for test generation has to be provided as per the guidelines defined in the proposed framework. Framework will customize the design model by taking the necessary information from the test analyst.

5.3. Test Generation

A test management criterion called test scenario that consists of test selection, requirement priority, test priority and test oracles will be generated from the model and requirements annotated by the test analyst. Semantics of the test cases will be considered and defined in the next stages of the research. Test scenario along with the requirements and the models will be used for generating the tests. That means the priorities defined in the test scenario will be later used for test generation and test execution. Suppose a user wants to execute all the tests with higher priority, then it is possible by defining the adequate test scenario. A traceability matrix will be generated that traces requirements to models and the generated tests. See test generation in Figure 2.

5.4. Test Execution & Analysis

Generated tests from the models will be executed and the test results will be generated for further analysis. See test execution and analysis in Figure 2.

6. Conclusion and Further Work

Proposed framework offers different advantages that include early detection of finding architectural, specification and design failures before implementation. A major contribution of the our research is to define and develop a framework, methodological guidance to facilitate model based testing as major part of the software development process by providing solutions for the problems defined above.

In the future, a framework will be developed (See Figure 2) which facilitates requirement specification, modelling, test management, test generation, test execution and test analysis. A case study will be carried out to prove the efficiency and effectiveness of the framework. The degree of completeness of the solution will be analysed and measured based on the case study.

7. References

Andrews, A., France, R. B., Ghosh, S. and Craig, G. (2003), "Test adequacy criteria for UML design models", Software Testing, Verification Reliability, vol. 13

Bertolino, A. (2007), "Software testing research: Achievements, challenges, dreams" FOSE '07: 2007 Future of Software Engineering. IEEE Computer Society.

Bertolino, A., Marchetti, E., and Muccini, E. (2005), "Introducing a Reasonably Complete and Coherent Approach for Model- Based Testing", Electronic notes in theoretical Computer Science.

Bringmann, E., and Kraemer, A. (2008), "Model-based Testing of Automotive Systems",2008 International Conference on Software Testing, Verification, and Validation.

Cavarra, A, and Chrichton, C. (2000), "Using UML for Automatic Test Generation", Oxford University Computing Laboratory, Tools and Algorithms for the Construction and Analysis of Systems.

Dai, Z.R., (2004), "Model-driven testing with UML 2.0.", Fraunhofer FOKUS, Berlin, Germany.

Dalal, S.R., Jain, A., Karunanithi, N. Leaton, J.M., Lott, C.M., Patton, G.C and Horowitz, B.M. (1999), "Model-Based Testing in Practice" ICSE 1999.

Dias Neto, A., Subramanyan, A. R. , Vieira, M., and Tracassos, G. (2007) "A survey on model-based testing approaches: A systematicreview," Siemens Corporate Research, Tech. Rep., 2007.

Emanuela, G.C, Franciso, G.O., and Patricia, D.L.M. (2007), " Test Case Generation by means of UML Sequence Diagrams and Labeled Transition Systems", Systems, Man and Cybernetics, 2007. ISIC.

Legeard, B. (2010), "Model-based Testing: a new paradigm for manual and automated functional testing", Testing Experience magazine, March 2010.

Mc Quillan, J.A. and Power, J.F. (2005), "A Survey of UML Based Coverage Criteria for Software Testing," Department of Computer Science, Tech. Rep.

Mingsong, C. (2006), " Automatic test case generation for UML activity diagrams", AST '06: Proceedings of the 2006 international workshop on Automation of software test.

Naslavsky, L. (2007), " Towards traceability of model-based testing artifacts", Proceedings of the 3rd international workshop on Advances in model-based testing, 2007.

Offutt, J. and Abdurazik, A. (1999), " Generating Tests from UML Specifications", George Mason University, Fairfax VA 22030, USA.

Offutt, J. and Abdurazik, A. (2000), "Using UML Collaboration diagrams for static checking and test generation", Third International Conference on UML in York, UK.

Prasanna.M and Chandran,K.R. (2009) Automatic Test Case Generation for UML Object diagrams using Genetic Algorithm, ICSRS Publication

Samuel, P., Mall, R. And Bothra A.K. (2008), "Automatic Test Case Generation Using UML State Diagrams".

Sarma, M. and Mall,R. (2007), "Automatic Test Case Generation from UML Models", 10th International Conference on Information Technology

Soldal, M. (2006), "Deriving tests from UML 2.0 sequence diagrams with neg and assert" AST '06: Proceedings of the 2006 international workshop on Automation of software test.

UML Testing Profile, (2009). http://utp.omg.org

Utting, M. and Legeard, B. (2007), "Practical Model-Based Testing: A Tools Approach. Morgan Kaufmann"

Utting, M., Pretchner, A. and Legeard, B. (2006), "A Taxonomy of Model Based Testing , a white paper."

Vieira, M., Leduc, J., Hasling, B., Subramanyan, R. and Kazmeier, J. (2006)"Automation of GUI testing using a modeldriven approach," in AST '06: Proceedings of the 2006 international workshop on Automation of software test.

Zander, J., Dai, Z.R., Schieferdecker, I. and Din, G. (2005). "From U2TP models to executable tests with TTCN-3 -an approach to model driven testing", Fraunhofer FOKUS, Berlin, Germany.

Zave, P. (1997), "Classification of research efforts in requirements engineering, " Computing Surveys (CSUR)" , Volume 29 Issue 4.

A New Architectural-Approach for Next Generation Automotive Applications

M.Glaab[1,2], W.Fuhrmann[1], J.Wietzke[1] and B.V.Ghita[2]

[1]Faculty of Computer Science, University of Applied Sciences Darmstadt, Germany
[2]Centre for Security, Communications and Network Research,
University of Plymouth, United Kingdom
{m.glaab, w.fuhrmann, j.wietzke}@fbi.h-da.de; bogdan.ghita@plymouth.ac.uk

Abstract

The automotive FM-tuner has evolved to a headunit which provides various functionalities to the passengers, e.g. navigation, audio/video-player and car-control functions. The customer demands are further increased by current smartphone and personal computer capabilities. Hence the development of appropriate architectures for the next generation of automotive applications, which facilitate such enhanced functionality, is a current research topic. As new applications in general require more hardware capabilities the traditional approach of integrating more and more functionalities into a powerful 'thick' headunit causes difficulties. With respect to the longer operating lifetime of vehicles, compared to most consumer electronic products, the hardware capabilities are becoming a bottleneck for the integration of future functionalities. This paper proposes an alternative approach to cope with that issue by use of an application delivery platform, accessed via wireless networks. In addition, requirements for wireless access networks are identified and first estimations on performance are made.

Keywords

Vehicle Communication, C2X, Automotive, Infotainment, Web of Services

1. Introduction

During the last decade the software embedded in cars has increased exponentially. Today's premium cars have more than 10 million lines of code distributed over up to 70 Electronic Control Units (ECUs) (Broy, 2006). The FM-tuner has evolved to a general-purpose headunit which integrates more and more functionalities such as navigation, phone, audio/video-player and also car-control functions (e.g. air-conditioning, driving-mode). The customers have demands for the same variety and flexibility of functionalities on next generation of automotive applications as they are used to having on their personal computers and smartphones. The architectures of the next in-car infotainment systems have to facilitate those. Additional functionalities in general require more computational power and memory. This poses a problem for the traditional approach of integrating new applications into the headunit ('thick headunit' approach) - especially in respect to the long lifetime of cars.

In this paper a new architectural approach of a thin headunit as a solution for the next generation automotive applications is proposed. This approach utilizes the fact that many new functionalities come along with mobile internet connection of the vehicle.

This paper is structured as follows: At first two basic architectural alternatives will be discussed. Beginning with the traditional thick headunit approach this paper motivates a new thin headunit approach. Afterwards first assumptions on the impacts of requirements regarding the wireless access network are made.

2. Architectural alternatives

As depicted, there is a high demand for new innovative or improved automotive applications. Thus future architectures for headunits have to facilitate innovative functionalities. Similar to personal computers and smartphones the fast and easy adding of applications during lifetime is requested. Also continuous update mechanisms for maintenance purposes are necessary. Two basic alternative architectural approaches will be discussed in the following: thick and thin headunit. This paper focuses on the technical problems which have to be solved and does not discuss cost issues. It is well understood that the wireless access and the storage of data in the network need very strong security protection, but security will not be discussed in detail within this paper.

2.1. Thick headunit

A thick headunit constitutes the continuation of the traditional development approach. It integrates more and more functionality, by installing new software applications. For that purpose AppStores, already known from actual smartphones, are currently discussed (Grunert, 2009) as mechanisms to provide new functionalities to the customers. Because of the historically highly specialised software of headunits (Pretschner et al., 2007), new operating systems, respectively software frameworks, are under development to facilitate open and individual automotive headunits. Examples are the Android based AutoLinQ or MeeGo.

Nevertheless, the integration of new functionalities into the headunit during its lifetime generally increases the requirements against the hardware. At least more memory is needed, but most of the enhanced applications also require more computational power. The studies showed that current headunits in many use-cases already working at their full CPU load with their factory range of functions. Therefore the hardware capabilities of headunits are an issue that has to be considered while discussing next generation of automotive software. These circumstances intensify if the average age of cars is taken into account. While consumer electronic products like smartphones and personal computers are usually replaced every 2-3 years, the vehicles in Germany have an average age of 8 years (KBA, 2010) and the OEMs have to maintain the vehicle at least 15 years.

Innovative automotive software is not only a requirement related to software architecture. By continuing the traditional approach of thick and powerful headunits, concepts for upgrading and replacing the headunits' hardware are required. Those difficulties motivate an alternative approach which will be discussed subsequently.

2.2. Thin headunit

Future innovative automotive software applications are accompanied by connecting the vehicle to the internet. Fully aware of the challenges for such network connections like high and variable vehicle velocities, tunnels etc. it can be expected that the capabilities of wireless access networks are continuously rising, which motivates the new approach of a 'thin headunit'. The basic idea is moving functionalities from the in-car domain into a centralized application delivery platform, accessed through a communication network (see figure 1).

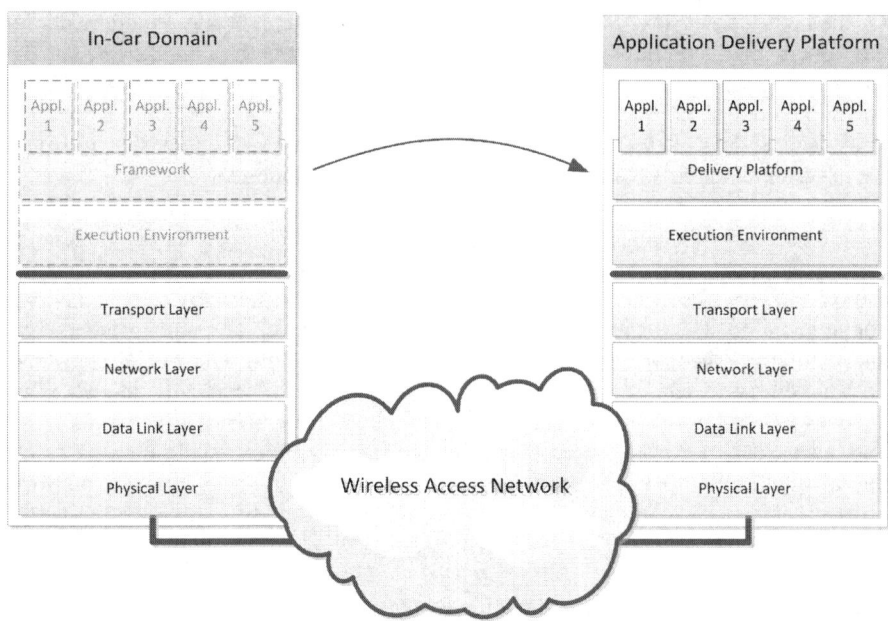

Figure 1: Abstract network-layer-centric view

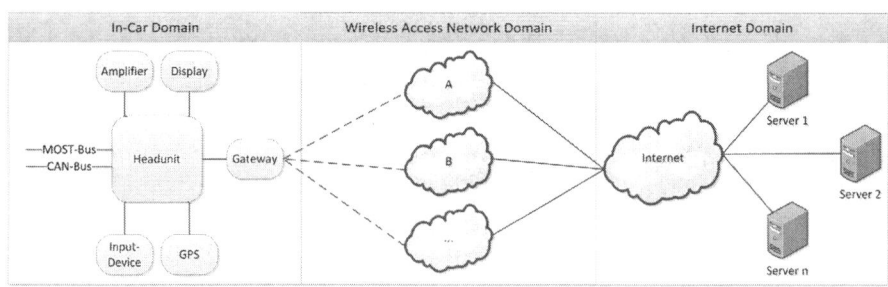

Figure 2: Overall technical architecture view

13

More precisely, the in-car applications are provided by one or many server(s) and have to be accessed via wireless access networks (see figure 2). The remaining headunit is a thin terminal, connecting the in-car display, speakers, input devices, and internal bus-systems to the access network.

This approach moves computational- and memory-intensive functionalities to the web, where it can be assumed that 'infinite' processing and storage resources are available and processing is well organized and managed. Having the most dynamic parts of the embedded infotainment system outside the in-car domain makes it easier to add new applications after market launch, meaning during the systems' lifetime since the hardware capabilities of the headunit have less significance. For example if an enhanced 3D-navigational map requires 200 MHz more computational power – just add it to the server. If the passenger would like to have 10 GBytes more memory for his audio files – just add it to the server. In both examples the requirements for the in-car part of the system remain constant: Displaying an enhanced 3D-navigational map requires transferring the screen with a defined resolution, frame rate and colour depth. Playing an audio-file means transferring one audio-stream per time, independent of the amount of tracks contained within an audio library. Hence the need for headunit's hardware upgrade becomes less important.

Beside use-cases for vehicles as service consumers, use-cases as service generators are currently investigated in many research projects dealing with advanced traffic safety and traffic efficiency scenarios. The generic term is c2x (car-to-x) communication which stands for the communication of vehicles among themselves and with infrastructure e.g. traffic lights. While sensitive traffic safety services may be handled by means of highly specialised communication technologies, all other services are supposed to be handled via public wireless access networks. This approach offers a new view on the discussed c2x scenarios: Realisation of safety uncritical use-cases as applications within a centralized application delivery platform turns many c2x communication scenarios into 'simple' server to server communication scenarios.

Further, the realisation of next generation automotive applications using a centralized application delivery platform improves maintainability, because the servers can be accessed at any time. Software updates can be performed immediately without physical access to the vehicles.

The new thin headunit approach in particular generates requirements to the wireless access network. First rough assumptions are depicted in the following.

3. Wireless Access Network Requirements

For the thin headunit approach the wireless access network is the enabling technology. It has to ensure that the services, provided by a centralized application delivery platform, can be used in the vehicle with a suitable quality. It has to be investigated, how a wireless access can be provided, which is sufficiently stable and provides sufficient capacity for transporting the required mixed communication traffic. A first rough approximation of uplink and downlink traffic, offered for selected use-cases, is given in the following.

3.1. Bandwidth

A central requirement for the wireless access network is to provide sufficient bandwidth and stability for the applications. The required bandwidth is being considered separately for the uplink-/downlink directions. At this stage we do not yet consider a specific wireless access technology and therefore we neglect additional load, such as protocol overhead.

3.1.1. Upload per headunit

With a thin headunit, which does not perform any pre-filtering, all information on the connected internal bus systems have to be uploaded. The CAN (Controller Area Network) is common for infotainment and car management purposes. Depending on the OEM and vehicle series it operates with speeds up to 125 Kbit/s which therefore can be assumed as necessary upload bandwidth. Since all input devices are connected to this bus, the application control data is already covered as well as the geographical position, the speed, the heading and other vehicular information related to service generation use-cases.

For some special use-cases like speech recognition for headunit control commands or navigational destinations, an additional 192 kBit/s for audio upload with MP3 or AAC codec is needed temporarily.

3.1.2. Download per headunit

For modern infotainment systems an 8 inch display with a resolution of 800x600 pixels can be assumed. All displayed data has to be received via the wireless access network. The hardest requirement is to display a video, because of the necessary high frame rate. For a DVD video with a resolution of 752x480 pixels (nearly fullscreen), making use of an actual video codec like h.264, at least 1 Mbit/s can be assumed. In case of displaying simple configuration menus mechanisms comparable to VNC (Virtual Network Computing) respectively RDP (Remote Desktop Protocol) may perform well. They show adequate results with much less than 1 Mbit/s on average (Yang et al., 2002).

Furthermore audio data such as navigational announcements or music have to be transmitted. Current MP3 or AAC codecs are providing good results with bandwidths from 128 kbit/s through to 192 kbit/s. Latest codecs already enable surround sound at those bitrates (Rose et al., 2008).

Finally some application data has to be transferred to the internal bus systems. As previously described the CAN works with speeds up to 125 kbit/s. Since many ECUs are connected to this bus, the share of the headunit is assumed to be 20 kbit/s on average.

15

3.1.3. Total per headunit

The given assumptions lead to a necessary bandwidth of approximately 1.5 Mbit/s downstream and 0.5 Mbit/s upstream per vehicle. This bandwidth also has to be available while the vehicle is moving, even with high speeds up to 250 kph.

3.1.4. Assumptions per wireless access network cell

Assuming that every vehicle has a thin headunit the wireless access network has to provide a multiple of the per vehicle bandwidth within a certain area. The total available bandwidth of the wireless access network within a wireless cell is divided by all of its members. The highest vehicle density occurs in city or traffic jam scenarios, where many vehicles are driving with quite low speed and hence small inter-vehicle-space. Assume a 6-lane motorway traffic jam scenario, where approximately 5 m long vehicles are driving with an average speed of 10 kph with an assumed inter-vehicle-space of 5 m. This leads to 600 vehicles per 1000 m motorway. If 25 percent of all vehicles are using a thin headunit the wireless access network has to provide up to 225 Mbit/s of download-bandwidth and up to 75 Mbit/s of upload bandwidth per 1000 m cell size.

3.2. Further requirements

Beside the bandwidth the wireless access network has to meet further requirements to enable the proposed thin headunit approach. The most important ones are briefly presented in the following. Since several decades of research, it is well known that mobile radio channels are unreliable, varying with time and location (Jakes et al., 1994; Hata 1980; Parson 1992; Rappaport 1996), are absolutely limited by the allocated radio spectrum and require special procedures for accessing the common medium (Goodman 1989; Fuhrmann 1994).

Bit error ratio: Average bit error ratio is much higher than in wired access networks. This requires strong forward and backward error correction procedures, depending on the application.

Latency, Jitter: Some applications are delay critical and require fast responses, e.g. speech recognition, voice calls, user interactions. They need low latency of the wireless access network. Especially audio applications need a low variance in delay (jitter). As different applications may run in parallel (e.g. voice call and navigation) adequate Quality of Service (QoS) profiles have to be accessible to provide an appropriate network quality.

Coverage: Vehicles are able to reach far-off areas, tunnels etc. The discussed approach demands for an adequate coverage of the accessible areas.

Seamless handovers: Handovers between different wireless access network cells or technologies have to be seamless by means of no disruption of the ongoing communication occurs.

Security, Privacy: The transmission of vehicle data e.g. the current geographic position and speed is sensitive. The networks and application server delivery platforms have to provide secure communication. Further mechanisms have to be applied to protect the users' privacy (also referred to as informational self-determination).

New wireless standards, such as Long Term Evolution / System Architecture Evolution (LTE/SAE) of 3GPP (Holma et al., 2009; Olsson et al., 2009) define a wireless access framework, which in combination with other wireless technologies potentially provide the necessary functional building blocks to realize the proposed wireless access approach.

4. Conclusions and Outlook

It has been shown that there is a demand for innovative automotive applications. Motivated by the issue of rising hardware limitations for new applications regarding to the traditional software architecture, a thin headunit approach was proposed. This approach, however, requires intensive wireless communication between cars and fixed infrastructure.

Future research activities have to detail those requirements and have to analyse how wireless access networks can meet them. These issues will be investigated using practical experiments in the in-car multimedia lab in Darmstadt and using extensive simulation. The simulations will be carried out using ns-3 (ns-3, 2010) where we have started adding required modules.

It has to be further investigated how applications for the application delivery platform have to be designed for most effective network utilisation. Depending on those results some use-cases might be identified that have to be solved inside the car because of their special requirements. Further, the realisation of in-car applications on centralized application delivery platforms potentially generates privacy and security issues. Related threats have to be identified.

5. References

Broy, M. (2006), *"Challenges in automotive software engineering"*, In: Proceedings of the 28th International Conference on Software Engineering, p. 33–42, New York, NY, USA, ACM.

Fuhrmann W., Brass V. (1994), *"Performance aspects of the GSM radio subsystem"*, In: Proceedings of the IEEE, Vol. 82, No. 9, pp.1449–1466

Goodman D., Valenzuela R., Gayliard K., Ramamurthi B. (1989), *"Packet reservation multiple access for local wireless communications"*, In: IEEE Transactions on Communications, Vol. 37, No. 8, pp. 885–890

Grunert, M. (2009), *"Grenzenlose Individualisierung durch BMW ConnectedDrive. Infotainment der Zukunft: Concept BMW Application Store"*, http://www.pressebox.de/pressemeldungen/bmw-group/boxid/288323 (Accessed 4 August 2010)

Hata M. (1980), *"Empirical formula for propagation loss in land mobile radio services"*, In: IEEE Transactions on Vehicular Technology, Vol. 29, No. 3, pp.317–325

Holma H., Toskala A. (2009), *"LTE for UMTS-OFDMA and SC-FDMA Based Radio Access"*, Wiley

Jakes W., Cox D. (1994), *"Microwave mobile communications"*, Wiley-IEEE Press

KBA (2010), http://www.kba.de/cln_016/nn_125264/DE/Statistik/Fahrzeuge/Bestand/bestand__node.html?__nnn=true#rechts (Accessed 6 August 2010)

Ns-3 (2010), http://www.nsnam.org (Accessed 23 September 2010)

Olsson M., Sultanan S., Rommer S., Frid L., Mulligan C. (2009), *"System Architecture Evolution (SAE): Evolved Packet Core for LTE, Fixed and Other Wireless Accesses"*, Academic Press

Parsons J.D. (1992), *"The mobile radio propagation channel"*, Halsted Press

Pretschner, A., Broy, M., Kruger, I. H. and Thomas S. (2007), *"Software engineering for automotive systems: A roadmap"*, In: International Conference on Software Engineering 2007, p. 55-71, Washington, DC, USA, IEEE.

Rappaport T.S. (1996), *"Wireless communications: principles and practice"*, Prentice-Hall, NJ

Rose, M., Nordmann, J. (2008), *"MPEG Surround – A Bright New Future for Surround Sound"* In: Information Quarterly Magazine, Vol. 7, No. 4

Yang, S. J., Nieh, J., Selsky, M. and Tiwari, N. (2002), *"The Performance of Remote Display Mechanisms for Thin-Client Computing"*. In: Proceedings of the USENIX Annual Technical Conference, Montery, CA, USA

An Approach for Structuring Heterogeneous Automotive Software Systems by use of Multicore Architectures

A.Knirsch[1,2], J.Wietzke[1], R.Moore[1] and P.S.Dowland[2]

[1]Faculty of Computer Science, University of Applied Sciences Darmstadt, Germany
[2]Centre for Security, Communications and Network Research,
University of Plymouth, United Kingdom
{a.knirsch, j.wietzke, r.moore}@fbi.h-da.de, pdowland@plymouth.ac.uk

Abstract

The significance of software within modern cars increases continuously. A manufacturer's competitive advantage relies more and more on compelling functionalities provided to the passengers. This raises the pressure on software architects of electronic automotive components. The successful integration of different software becomes a major challenge. This paper presents an approach to give support on that issue by the use of multicore hardware architectures. By reflecting the internal structure of the software in the underlying hardware, the scheduling of tasks performed in parallel can be determined based on the internal architecture rather than on performance aspects only.

Keywords

Multicore, Integration, Automotive, Parallel Development, Thread Affinity

1. Introduction

Modern cars are equipped with infotainment systems providing various services to the passengers. When observing current developments within the domain of such In-Car Multimedia (ICM) systems, an increasing amount of integrated functionalities can be noticed. The legacy radio within the dashboard has already merged with navigational and telephone devices. It provides capabilities to render video and audio media. To download add-on information, it is permanently connected to cellular networks and is able to synchronise content with mobile devices. This evolution affects the complexity of such highly integrated software systems, which causes a demand for software frameworks supporting the application developers. Such support has effects on the development duration and the quality of the product (Wietzke and Tran, 2005).

The use of a well-tested and approved framework facilitates an effective internal structuring of the software system. But a framework is only of limited use for a concurrent software development process, as long as it fails to provide support for the integration of different software. In this context 'different' is related to internal structure, priority models, vendor, or resource utilisation. An objective of this research is the development of a comprehensive software framework to improve the integration of software for embedded systems in the context of ICM devices.

1.1. Peculiarities of software development within automotive domains

The automotive sector has to consider several constraints which are relevant for building software systems (Pretschner et al., 2007). This includes the heterogeneous nature of the software, reaching from entertainment to safety and time critical control functions. Those are distributed across several connected Electronic Control Units (ECU) with interdependencies between them. The increasing amount of software within modern vehicles exposes the characteristics of complex IT systems. To keep the number of ECUs at a manageable size and in order to meet requirements regarding power consumption, space, weight and of course cost, more and more functionalities have to be combined and integrated. Additionally the amount of variants and different configurations has to be reflected by the software architecture. The resulting artefact can be compared with very large scale integration (VLSI) on the software level.

With 15 years and longer the lifetime exceeds those found with software systems in other domains, whereas the capabilities for maintenance are limited. Further the software engineering inherited the division of labour from the mechanical engineering of the automotive domain: each major component is designed and delivered by a different company. This causes increased efforts and risks for the integration of the targeted systems. The development process has to be coordinated independently of geographical borders, linguistic barriers, and specific domain knowledge while rendering a highly integrated system. This problem is going to be multiplied with respect to the expectations propagated by Volkmar Denner (CEO Robert Bosch GmbH) during his keynote speech at the Automotive Electronics 2010 in Ludwigsburg, telling that many non-automotive applications are going to be deployed into vehicles. Such statements are based on his perception that consumer electronics with its fast design cycles and short product lifetimes, is influencing the in-car environment, which will affect the entire design chain (Hammerschmidt, 2010).

1.2. Multicore architectures

Multicore (MC) architectures have been common in the high performance computing (HPC) sector for decades. In the recent past they have emerged and proved applicability also in server and desktop market segments, to solve the need for more computational power while improving energy efficiency. This is mainly driven by the fact that the increase of clock speeds to improve performance reached a physical barrier due to current limits in transistor technologies. This is also valid for the domain of embedded systems, where special purpose cores support the main processing unit to form a heterogeneous system-on-chip (SoC) MC architecture. But also homogeneous MC architectures are already available for different instruction set architectures (Levy and Conte, 2009). Those provide a number of advantages, some of the most prominent of which are outlined in (Smit et al., 2008) as follows:

Scalability is supported, as the architecture itself does not grow in complexity with future technologies. Only the number of provided computational cores increases, depending on the density of the integrated circuits and the size of the silicon. The computational power of MC CPUs scales linearly with the number of integrated cores, although the exploitation will suffer slightly due to necessary overhead.

Energy efficiency can be obtained by switching off unused cores to reduce the static power consumption. Also the clock speed might be dynamically adapted to current needs for computation tasks which do not have to fulfil hard real-time constraints for determinism. Energy efficiency increases with reduced clock speeds, resulting in a lower thermal footprint.

Independency of computational tasks is realised by space division on MC architectures in contrast to the time division manner of multitasked software systems executing on single-core systems. That means that MC systems support a parallel processing whereas single-core systems have to perform jobs concurrently ('as if they were parallel'). MC systems still have to compete for shared resources. Functional dependencies are realised by using an inter-core communication network for routing information between the cores, also referred to as network-on-chip (NoC).

As well as the benefits of this new stage of parallelism in embedded systems, there are also some drawbacks. To utilise the facilities of multiple cores, the applications to be applied have to address the issues of software executed in parallel (Cantril and Bonwick, 2008). Eventually MC CPUs were basically introduced to avoid the physical problem of increasing clock-speeds to enhance computational power and not as a new feature to provide more parallelism, which the software developers have to cope with. But nevertheless MC architectures do provide an opportunity to reflect a parallel software design in hardware, as presented below.

The following section focuses on hardware architectures utilising multiple homogeneous processing cores, sharing a common accessible memory region connected by a NoC that supports multiple concurrent communications utilised by an Portable Operating System Interface for Unix (POSIX) conform operating system (OS), which does support symmetric multiprocessing (SMP).

This paper is structured as follows:

- Section 2 develops the need for a new approach for a software framework supporting the integration of heterogeneous software. The example of an ICM system is used for illustrative reasons.

- Section 3 defines a set of architectural drivers, which have impact on the internal structure of a heterogeneous software system. Further a basic approach is presented that utilises the qualities of MC processors. Within that context, the focus is set on the support for integration of software systems in order to ease the creation of a homogeneous whole.

- Section 4 summarises and provides an outlook for further research.

2. The need for a new software integration approach

Within the automotive domain the Original Equipment Manufacturers (OEM) obtain almost all of the electronic components, including the software, from suppliers (tier-one OEMs). These have to meet the requirements and design specifications with respect to the interfaces defined by the OEMs. This implies that theoretically all the components forming the distributed system within a certain car are compatible to the predefined rules and therefore are also compatible with the Electronic Control Units (ECU) they depend on. Although all parties agree to a common set of specifications, the increasing amount of functionalities incorporated into such distributed systems causes a lack of predictability regarding the compatibility. The maintainability as well as the capabilities to identify the root causes for unexpected behaviour decrease (Sangiovanni-Vincentelli and Di Natale, 2007). Although the reasons for those problems could be denominated as organisational or communication problems during the development process, a solution on that level is not foreseeable due to incongruent interests of the involved parties. A supplier usually is only able to provide a competitive offer as long as the efforts necessary can be reused for multiple clients. Therefore the agreed specifications are good and necessary but seldom sufficient for a predictable integration. The supplier has not necessarily much interest in easing the integration efforts of the OEM if his own return of investment will suffer. That approach leads to the situation as depicted by Sangiovanni-Vincentelli and Di Natale:

> "The integration of subsystems is done routinely, albeit in a heuristic and ad hoc way. The resulting lack of an overall understanding of the subsystems' interplay, and the difficulties encountered in integrating very complex parts, make systems integration a very challenging job."
> (Sangiovanni-Vincentelli and Di Natale, 2007, p. 42)

Based on the experience gained through an inter-institutional co-operation with a tier-one OEM of ICM devices, it is assumed it is not possible to adequately specify a system in advance with currently available design techniques. For example it can be questioned how to express the load behaviour of a software (sub-)system on different task priorities. This is particularly necessary by subsystems which actively and autonomously change their task's prioritisations to circumvent the need for explicit synchronisation by use of semaphores and mutual exclusions. The same is valid for ones which adapt with dynamic prioritisation changes to current system utilisation by use of latency measurements between tasks' change from 'ready' to 'running' state. Integration of such software can't be performed routinely, which applies even more if it is provided as binary.

One single supplier historically provides one ECU. It is contained in a separate box that is connected to sensors, actuators, and at least one field bus system of the in-car communication network. That box reacts to the input given by sensors and messages received through the in-car communication network. With increasing variability the complexity increases due to the also increasing number of combinations of valid system setups. This also applies for user-event driven systems which communicate with ECUs. A modern ICM system provides a good example for a software system relying on interdependencies with internal and external control units. Such units form logical sub-domains, supporting the abstraction of the overall complexity as outlined in figure 1. An integration of the domains implies the shared use of system resources.

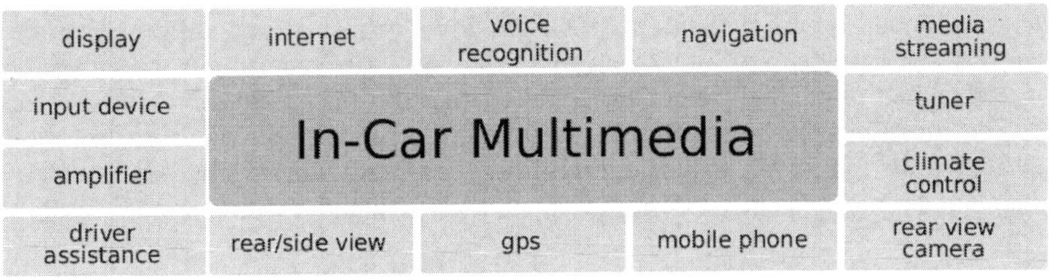

display	internet	voice recognition	navigation	media streaming
input device				tuner
amplifier	In-Car Multimedia			climate control
driver assistance	rear/side view	gps	mobile phone	rear view camera

Figure 1: Exemplary domains of an ICM system

The vertical separation of the overall system functionality into ECUs to be integrated by the OEM is derived from the automotive mechanical engineering production process. If the content of a system is driven by the complexity and extent of the architectural drivers, it is an appropriate solution to parallelise the development process. By dividing a system into distinct parts, the resulting pieces can be handled independently as long as the interfaces of the arising modules are sufficiently defined. That strategy implies the coordination of a concurrent development process with a large number of parties and interests involved (Pretschner et al., 2007).

The tier-one OEMs adopt that 'approved' policy and alter from producer to integrators, as the 'car manufacturers' changed to 'car integrators' within the last decades. They also separate their targeted systems into subsystems, to be developed concurrently by independent software engineering teams within, as well as outside their organisation. In some cases the integrator is even able to make use of already existing components, originally targeted for a different purpose. In result, the development process follows the system's functionalities' breakdown structure. That way the process scales with the system complexity, but inherits the complexity derived by the dependencies between independent development teams of interdependent software components.

In contrast to the network of different (loosely coupled) ECUs, which basically share one (or more) common communication media, the software subsystems of a single ECU have to share all the resources provided by the underlying hardware. This includes computational power, memory, and access to external interfaces like the in-car communication network. The use of these has to be coordinated. For such highly integrated systems this can be realised by a priority based scheduling, supported through an underlying OS. By use of given priorities assigned to each task, the scheduler decides which one is allowed to compute and implicitly can have access to available hardware resources. A widely accepted scheduling algorithm is 'round robin' (POSIX: SCHED_RR) which grants each scheduled task up to a fixed time quantum before it is replaced (pre-emptive scheduling) by the next queued task that holds the highest priority. While the situation is more complex for SMP and MC systems, the decision on what to compute next is still essentially based on priorities.

Due to the concurrent development process, the system's components are developed in a simplified environment not including all interdependencies of the targeted system. But the tight coupling of the targeted system affects the behaviour and stability of implementations relying on concurrent execution on shared resources. A notable amount of ECU failures can be put down to insufficient software qualities causing not recoverable failing states (Broy, 2006). An enumeration of causes for errors related to parallel execution would contain for example dead- and live-locks due to insufficient thread safety and conflicting prioritisation. These can probably only be observed after the integration of all components, because they simply don't show up during an isolated development and testing (without shared resources).

Whereas the other causes for errors named above can be reduced to erroneous code, a conflicting prioritisation is more likely the result of inadequate communication during the implementation or insufficient specification during the design phase. Also the process of transferring the design to the implementation level, while utilising a task-based prioritisation could introduce deficiencies. On the design level certain priorities could be assigned to given use-cases and activities, which derived system components have to follow (e.g. a phone component might have to follow different priorities than a radio tuner component, especially when receiving a phone call). Additionally, components might use an internal priority scheme, due to the fact that internal activities also vary on importance – probably also related to the current state of the overall system. Ideally, healthy cooperation and/or management would ensure that a commonly agreed upon scheme eases the integration process. But, driven by issues of cost-efficiency, not only special purpose software but also OTS (off-the-shelf) and legacy parts have to be integrated. Those do not have to follow a commonly agreed scheme, due to a completely independent development (Pellizzoni and Caccamo, 2007).

Under the assumption that the complexity of automotive software systems is increasing continuously, which has an impact on the number of subsystems, the predictability of necessary integration efforts gains importance. The following section depicts how the integration process of highly interdependent software systems can be stabilised to improve predictability by use of MC hardware architectures.

3. Defining self-contained execution domains

When beginning to structure a system with predefined functionality where the architect possesses all degrees of freedom (no predefined architectural restrictions, OTS software or legacy code to consider), it is suitable to decompose the functionality into fine-grained separate tasks using software engineering techniques to transfer abstract functionality to implementation level. In this context a task is defined as the smallest schedulable execution item, like a thread in QNX Neutrino RTOS (Real-Time OS) or GNU/Linux OS. Based on certain constraints they can be partitioned into groups of tasks. Those can be agglomerated into execution domains, which can be mapped to the available computational cores as illustrated in figure 2. The constraints can be derived from the attributes of the individual tasks in association with their interdependencies. An appropriate way is to differentiate the tasks and the related implementation (if already available) based on their internal architecture, their shared memory regions, their vendor (especially for OTS parts), and their lifecycle or ability to be reused. Considering those factors will lead to a generally coarser grained segmentation in comparison to a design with all degrees of freedom.

The internal dependencies can be rated by use of design structure matrices (DSM). Those reflect the amount, frequency and direction of information exchanged between tasks (Sangal et al., 2005). Such dynamic information most certainly will change during system operation. Therefore an adequate system profiling is advisable to achieve expressive and effective results.

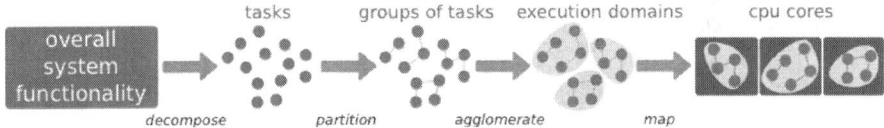

Figure 2: Decomposition and mapping on the hardware level

In the real world the decomposition and development commonly does not look like the process depicted in figure 2. To manage the complexity of the overall system, functionalities can be outlined using use-cases. Accompanied with further high-level design information the implementation can be separated into distinct chunks to be provided by suppliers. The task of the integrator is to unite the resulting chunks and arrange those onto the available hardware as depicted in figure 3. Architectural design concepts like use-cases, components and modules, for proper abstraction and modelling a system, help to cope with complexities. But the resulting design artefacts still have to be transferred to the level of implementation utilising the application programming interface (API) of the OS and programming languages.

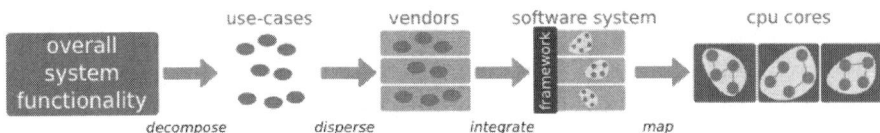

Figure 3: Decomposition and mapping on the system level

The performance of an integrated software system is highly dependent on efficient messaging and memory access. This is especially applicable for cost-efficient solutions which do not allow an extensive communication overhead introduced by an abstraction layer to support a loose coupling. Therefore inter-process communication (IPC) based on shared memory is still a method of choice in efficient environments opposed to more loosely coupled techniques. MC hardware architectures support this by coherent cache hierarchies to reduce memory access latencies by decreasing cache misses. That means the throughput can be improved when communication partners use a shared cache instead of the main memory. Information stored within shared caches can be accessed about 10 (or more) times faster than memory connected via system bus. An optimised arrangement of tasks can improve overall system performance (Tam, 2007). Therefore a sensible clustering of tasks on the CPU cores can be justified also for economical reasons when looking for time and space efficient solutions in terms of usage of computational and memory resources.

With SMP a single OS abstracts the hardware resources and employs a single scheduler to disperse computational resources based on predefined priorities. For a MC system this implies that tasks ready for computation are scheduled to available computational cores considering an equal dispersion of load while reflecting given priorities. Neither the constraints outlined above for grouping and bundling of tasks, nor the communication flows between the tasks influence this distribution. In best case a scheduler keeps a task on a particular core as long as possible to reduce cache bouncing effects. Cache bouncing increases cache invalidations which cause read and write misses and therefore rising latencies during memory access (Tam, 2007).

With the objective to ease the integration of heterogeneous software by utilising MC architectures, a software framework reflecting the depicted peculiarities improves usability. Such a system should be able to mitigate risks caused by unforeseeable integration expenses and thus help to predict the success of development projects. For the successful isolation of execution domains a set of essential capabilities has to be provided by an underlying framework in association with the utilised OS.

- Tasks and groups of them can be bound to certain predefined CPU cores.
- That binding is inherited to dynamically created sub-tasks by default.
- The scheduler supports the parallel execution of tasks, which make use of different priorities on different computational cores.
- The static mapping of tasks to cores appears transparent to the application developers and is managed only by the system integrator.

The capabilities given above constitute the minimum to implement the proposed approach. Further features can provide more flexibility basically on the integration level as well as during runtime. For example a logical hierarchy of agglomerates provides capabilities to dynamically merge and split groups of tasks to adapt to current computational needs for efficient resource utilisation.

The enabling technology for the approach is thread affinity (Love, 2003; Nagarajan and Nicola, 2009). The computational cores are addressable by use of bit-masks. With this feature the system scheduler is ordered to schedule a particular task only for computational cores matching the defined bit-mask. This introduces the dimension of space, beside priority and which task was queued first in the waiting line. Thus an integrator can define for any given agglomerate which core (or group of cores) the contained tasks are allowed to be computed on. He is enabled to define an execution domain in form of a dedicated core by adapting the scheduler's allocations depending on implemented use-cases, independent of the software's internals. This applies also for agglomerates, which aren't available in source code.

This approach was incorporated into an embedded software framework, developed at the ICM-lab of the Faculty of Computer Science of the h_da - University of Applied

Sciences Darmstadt (OpenICM, 2010). First evaluations served as proof for the applicability and validity: The API for the application developer did not need to be changed, whereas the integrator is now empowered to cluster the components on certain CPU cores with minimal efforts (only one additional argument for indicating the targeted core is necessary for the subsystems start routine). The framework enables a system architect even to reuse components not targeted for parallel computation. Further it provides the capability to optimise cache performance for appropriate partitioned systems, due to the achievable reduction of unnecessary cache invalidations. The implementation scales very well with increasing complexity, simulated by an increasing number of different components.

As a result of such a static configuration, the tasks are scheduled as defined by the integrator based on the interdependencies and predefined characteristics, rather than 'only' depending on an equal dispersion of workload. That means different software (e.g. different by means of vendor, change rate, internal structure, internal priorities, mission) is separated. A task with high priority does not displace a low priority task, as long as both are defined for different execution domains (which implicitly means they could make use of different priority schemes). This probably doesn't support a most optimal performance, but improves the deterministic behaviour and helps to reach a higher grade of stability. Erroneous behaviour is not necessarily propagated beyond the boundaries of one computational core (or one set of computational cores predefined with a bit-mask). Depending on the implementation it is even possible to handle failures of affected subcomponents (Aggarwal et al., 2007).

Even more positive effects can be expected in terms of timely behaviour. The scheduler does not have to merge concurrent tasks of different software for one computational unit. Therefore a component behaves very similarly in timing as to what is observed when it is executed exclusively on a single-core system, similar to a separate ECU, as systems were designed in the past (but without additional housings, power supplies, etc.). Imminent conflicts are effectively reduced, without the need for changing the components internals.

4. Related Work

Other related research on integration is performed by Vergata et. al., which use the availability of the virtualisation capabilities of current hardware architectures to separate different software components. This approach effectively creates execution domains by use of virtual machines, not depending on a fixed number of CPU cores (Vergata et. al., 2010). Increased overhead to establish and run those machines has to be accepted.

QNX Software Systems provide the capability to partition software by use of resource budgets with their Adaptive Partitioning Scheduler (APS) (Johnson et. al., 2006). This scheduler relies on application specific policies (round robin, FIFO, etc.) and priorities, overlaid by configurable budgets (guaranteed portions) of system resources. Although each of those capabilities can provide benefits as long as utilised separately, a combination of all three has the potential to interfere with each other. Related research is currently performed at the ICM-lab of the h_da.

A great deal of research for structuring and govern complex software systems has been done in the field of service-oriented architectures. Automotive software systems do not pose an exception (Krueger et. al., 2004), but with improved abstraction of the complexity the overhead during runtime increases.

The OSGi Alliance propagates an open dynamic component platform to assure interoperability of applications and services. The platform addresses the integration issue of software provided by different vendors with respect to reliable operation, shared resources and the ability to add functionality during runtime. With a sophisticated service model it follows a service-oriented approach, relying on a Java Virtual Machine (JVM) (Kriens, 2008).

The approaches described above give support on the integration of heterogeneous software subsystems. An examination of the research work reveals the lack of efficient exploitation of the underlying hardware architecture or neglect issues caused through conflicting scheduling schemes and task prioritisation.

5. Conclusions and outlook

The increasing complexities within the automotive domain are historically countered by a divide and conquer strategy. This multi-branched recursion targeting on breaking down a problem into manageable parts was adapted by the software development approaches implemented by suppliers, and their subcontractors. These have to integrate heterogeneous software parts into a reliable and efficient system based upon a single hardware platform. But the concurrent implementation of sub-parts involves a high risk of an unpredictable integration process. This paper has demonstrated that this approach to utilise MC hardware architectures to retain the structure of the software system by use of defined execution domains is an appropriate way to mitigate that risk. It is lightweight enough to be usable in practice and proved practicalness by adopting it to an existing embedded software framework.

Essentially, this paper has identified problems related to software integration on the intersection of evolving MC architectures and automotive software systems. A main focus is set on the question of how flexible and reliable software frameworks can support the integration process. However, the problems of concurrency remain for unique peripheral resources shared by multiple computational resources. Therefore additional research is needed to determine the correct allocation and best parallel use of shared resources. Further research is necessary on how a system can be prioritised efficiently on design level, including a consideration on how to transfer such information to the implementation level. Another important question is how an appropriate partitioning of systems based on a system profiling can be achieved.

6. References

Aggarwal, N., Ranganathan, P., Jouppi, NP. and Smith, JE. (2007), *"Configurable Isolation: Building High Availability System with Commodity Multi-Core Processors"*, In: Proceedings of the 34th annual international symposium on Computer architecture, p. 470-481, ACM.

Broy, M. (2006), *"Challenges in automotive software engineering"*, In: Proceedings of the 28th International Conference on Software Engineering, p. 33–42, ACM.

Cantril, B. and Bonwick, J. (2008), *"Real-World Concurrency"*, In: ACM Queue, volume 6, issue 5, p. 16-25, ACM.

Hammerschmidt, C. (2010), *"Bosch sees massive challenges ahead for automotive electronics"*, Automotive Design Line.

Johnson, K., Clarke, J., Leroux, P. and Craig R. (2006) *"OS Partitioning for Embedded Systems"*, QNX Software Systems.

Kriens, P. (2008), *"How OSGi Changed My Life"*, In: ACM Queue, volume 6, issue 1, p. 44–51, ACM.

Krueger, IH., Nelson, EC. and Prasad, KV. (2004), *"Service-Based Software Development for Automotive Applications"*, In: Convergence International Congress & Exposition On Transportation Electronics, SAE International.

Levy, M. and Conte, TM. (2009), *"Embedded Multicore Processors and Systems"*, In: IEEE Micro, volume 29, issue 3, p. 7-9, IEEE.

Love, R. (2003), *"CPU Affinity"*. Linux Journal, volume 2003, issue 111, p. 8, Specialized Systems Consultants, Seattle, WA, USA.

Nagarajan, S. and Nicola, V. (2009), *"Processor Affinity or Bound Multiprocessing? Easing the Migration to Embedded Multicore Processing"*, QNX, Ottawa, Ontario, Canada.

OpenICM (2010), Webpage of the OpenICM Framework, h_da - University of Applied Sciences Darmstadt, Germany, http://openicm.fbi.h-da.de (last accessed 20-Aug-2010).

Pellizzoni, R. and Caccamo, M. (2007), *"Towards the Predictable Integration of Real-Time COTS Based Systems"*, In: Proceedings of the 28th IEEE Real-Time Systems Symposium, p. 73-82, IEEE.

Pretschner, A., Broy, M., Kruger, IH. and Thomas S. (2007), *"Software engineering for automotive systems: A roadmap"*, In: International Conference on Software Engineering 2007, p. 55-71, IEEE.

Sangal, N., Jordan, E., Sinha, V. and Jackson, D. (2005), *"Using dependency models to manage complex software architecture"*, In: Proceedings of the 20th annual conference on Object-oriented programming, systems, languages, and applications, p. 167-176, ACM.

Sangiovanni-Vincentelli, A. and Di Natale, M. (2007), *"Embedded System Design for Automotive Applications"*, In: Computer, volume 40, issue 10, p. 42–51, IEEE.

Smit, GJM., Kokkeler. ABJ., Wolkotte, PT. and van de Burgewal, MD. (2008) *"Multicore architectures and streaming applications"*, In: Proceedings of the 2008 International Workshop on System Level Interconnect Prediction, p. 35–42, ACM.

Tam, D., Azimi, R. and Stumm, M. (2007), *"Thread Clustering: Sharing-Aware Scheduling on SMP-CMP-SMT Multiprocessors"*, In: Proceedings of the 2nd European Conference on Computer Systems 2007, p. 47-58, ACM.

Vergata, S., Wietzke, J., Schütte, A., and Dowland, PS. (2010), *"System Design for Embedded Automotive Systems"*, In: Proceedings of the Sixth Collaborative Research Symposium on Security, E-learning, Internet and Networking (SEIN 2010), Plymouth.

Wietzke, J. and Tran, MT. (2005), *"Automotive Embedded Systeme"*, Xpert.press, Springer.

Towards a Classification of Information Technology Governance Frameworks

M.Krey[1,2], B.Harriehausen[1], M.Knoll[1] and S.M.Furnell[2]

[1] Darmstadt University of Applied Sciences, Darmstadt, Germany
[2] Centre for Security, Communications & Network Research,
University of Plymouth, Plymouth, United Kingdom.
e-mail: mike.krey@plymouth.ac.uk

Abstract

The issues, opportunities and challenges of effectively governing an organization's Information Technology (IT) demands and resources have become a major concern of the Board and executive management in many organisations today. The Swiss healthcare is currently searching for methods and practices for the solution of operational planning and optimisation of IT processes. To make sure that the corporate hospital strategy leads to adequate business decisions an IT GRC Framework for Healthcare will be needed. This paper presents the first task – the classification of existing IT governance frameworks – within the development process. After the dissociation of IT management and corporate governance – a proposal for a classification scheme for IT governance frameworks is described and the application of the classification template is explained.

Keywords

Governance, Risk, Compliance, Healthcare, Classification, Framework

1. Introduction

Governance, Risk Management and Compliance (GRC) is an executive level concern in many enterprises today. It is an approach that addresses not only the establishment of business rules but more importantly how those rules are integrated into sensible organisational structures, embedded into the day-to-day business processes of the organisation, communicated (including ongoing training) and monitored for compliance (Menzies, 2006). In this paper the GRC context governance means IT related governance and describes the topics that the executive management needs to address to govern IT within their hospital.

As ascertained by a survey with several Swiss hospital CIOs in 2009 the majority (64%) replied that the healthcare sector is a complex and heterogeneous economic sector and cannot be compared to other industry sectors where Control Objectives for Information and related Technology (CobiT) and other IT governance framework have been successfully applied. Organisational structures, legal restraints and over the years increased heterogeneous IT systems are just a few aspects which would make the healthcare sector a sensible field for the implementation of IT governance. It is pleasing to see that hospitals appear to be taking IT governance as a part of their governance realm and that 45% of the hospitals surveyed adopt IT Infrastructure

Library (ITIL) as an IT governance framework, while about 8% of hospitals have or will adopt CobiT, ISO-17799 or a proprietary framework. The majority believed that their ITIL approach is 'repeatable but intuitive', whilst no one thought their ITIL approach is 'fully optimised' and the processes have been refined to a level of good practice, based on the results of continuous improvement and maturity modeling with other hospitals (Krey et al., 2010).

To make sure that the corporate hospital strategy leads to adequate business decisions an IT GRC Framework for Healthcare will be needed. This framework can help to minimise risks and should consider the special requirements of the healthcare sector. The development of a healthcare specific IT GRC framework consists of three main phases. (1) Classification of existing IT governance frameworks. With the help of a classification scheme users as well as framework developers are provided with an overview of the framework e.g. relating to its addressed GRC area, framework design or framework application. (2) Exploration and systematisation of the factors influencing IT governance structures, processes and outcome and the requirements and expectations within the healthcare. To enhance the future reusability of such a framework, detailed information about the application method, requirements from the healthcare processes (business and IT), accessibility and levels of mutability are required. (3) Mapping of the existing IT governance frameworks and the derived requirements within the healthcare. This identifies a requirements overlap which can be fully or partly covered by the existing frameworks. In addition to it the mapping points out explicitly the gaps where healthcare specific requirements cannot be fulfilled with functionalities provided by the frameworks and where further research will be needed.

To give a widespread and lasting approach for IT governance in the healthcare sector, it is not sufficient to analyse only one framework like CobiT. Instead, it is necessary to complement it with the knowledge of other frameworks and the findings of academic research. This paper presents a classification system for IT governance frameworks. This task is discussed in the following sections. After the dissociation of IT management and corporate governance – a proposal for a classification scheme for IT governance frameworks is described and the paper ends with some concluding remarks.

2. IT Governance and IT Management

The difference between IT management and IT governance has been subject to confusion and myths in the IT community (van Grembergen, 2004; Johannsen et al., 2007). Peterson (2003) provides a clear insight into the differences between these two notions. "Whereas the domain of IT management focuses on the efficient and effective supply of IT services and products, and the management of IT operations, IT governance faces the dual demand of (1) contributing to present business operations and performance, and (2) transforming and positioning IT for meeting future business challenges". As depicted in figure 1, Peterson (2003) suggests positioning IT management and IT governance along two dimensions, business orientation and time orientation.

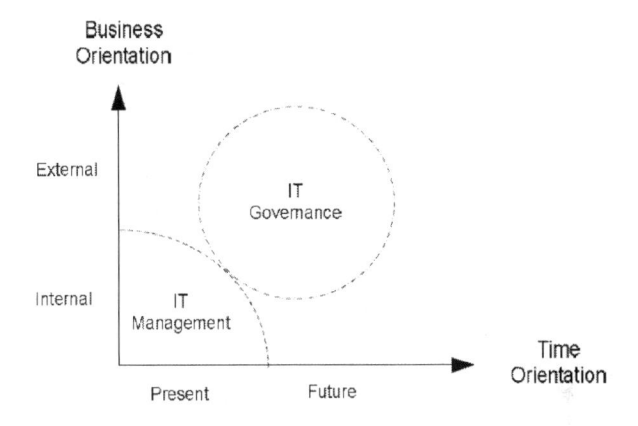

Figure 1: IT governance and IT management (Peterson, 2003)

Even today much of the literature does not differentiate IT management from IT governance. The two concepts are often regarded as synonymous, even though they clearly differ (Sohal and Fitzpatrick, 2002). An important key differentiator is that management tasks have an internal focus and are done at the departmental level, while IT governance is a corporate level activity with a purposeful external focus (Sohal and Fitzpatrick, 2002). Management is concerned with what kind of decisions are made, while governance is concerned with who should make decisions and how these decisions will be monitored. A change to an organisation's strategy may well require changes to the management but not the governance of an asset (Weill and Ross, 2007). In IT management, the provision of IT services and products can be assigned to an external provider (as in outsourcing), while IT governance is specific to an organisation. Since governance gives direction and control over IT expenditures, it cannot be outsourced and is the direct responsibility of the senior executive (Peterson, 2003).

3. IT Governance and Corporate Governance

Lee and Lee (2009) characterised IT governance by the attributes transparency, control, effectiveness and efficiency. Transparency and control are bequested by the discipline of corporate governance seeking to ensure the transparent management and control of IT assets through forms of committee. In other words they accentuate the integral part of an organisation to be represented in IT governance, however most researchers looks more narrowly to the processes of IT management than to the structure of IT organisations (Heier et al., 2007).

According to the literature, IT governance is concerned with the board's responsibility to ensure that the company's IT meets the present and future demands of the business and of the business's customers (Standards Australia, 2005; Peterson, 2003) and that the risks arising from IT are mitigated (Standards Australia, 2005; Cilli, 2003). It does this by assessing, directing and monitoring the company's IT to ensure that the required benefits and business outcomes are being achieved

(Standards Australia, 2005). Jordan and Silcock (2005) suggest that an organisation that is able to do this is "IT-capable" and summarise this capability in the following terms: "The board must be assured that the organisation is able to identify needs and opportunities to exploit IT, and is then able to satisfy them".

The Board is assisted in these tasks by the company's executive management and its IT management. According to van Grembergen and de Haes (2008) IT governance is practised at three levels within the organisation. These are:

- The strategic level, which they take to be the company board,
- The senior management level, and
- The operational management level.

All of these levels thus need to be addressed by any explanation of IT governance. Johnstone et al. (2006) propose that there are three components to IT governance. These are:

- An authority structure,
- A set of board policies, and
- A set of mechanisms or processes.

They note that the authority structure is that set up by the board to manage IT, which includes both appointments such as the IT manager and (often) an oversight committee. The board policies are those "decision guidelines and restraints" (Johnstone et al., 2006) devised by the board to control the use of IT in the company, including the business and IT strategies (p. 4).

4. Proposal for a Classification System

Several frameworks, reference models and best practices, issued by both international standardisation organisations and private organisations exist in addition to the de facto standard CobiT for managing the different aspects of IT and its organisation (Lahti and Peterson, 2005; IT Governance Institute, 2008; van Grembergen and de Haes, 2008; Johannsen et al., 2007; Addy, 2007).

A variety of approaches to classify IT governance frameworks can be found in academic literature.

- mostly a listing of the frameworks is provided,
- a detailed comparison of individual frameworks (Guldentops et al., 2010) can be found or
- sections of the frameworks are analysed by specific fields of application (e.g. IT security) (ISACA Switzerland Chapter, 1998).

Just a few approaches deal with the systematisation of frameworks, whereby it is the fact the tabulation of IT governance frameworks that is meant here and not so much the survey-like textual description of the actual stock of frameworks found in literature. The author conducted two parallel reviews, one focusing on the scientific literature and the other drawing on alternative sources available via the World Wide Web.

A couple of those approaches provide a deeper comparison of more than two models. Mostly the comparison is limited to the features of the model itself structured by abstract attributes without a deeper analysis of the provided scope of the process description (Walter and Krcmar, 2006). Based on this, there is also a lack of studies regarding the question of which framework or parts of it should be used in which situation. With regard to the purpose of this work an independent classification system for IT governance frameworks is needed. Whatever classification principle is used, the main problem in developing an appropriate classification lies in limiting the scope to as few descriptive characteristics as possible which should at the same time explain the diversity and be as mutually exclusive as possible. For this purpose the characteristic-based approach has been used to develop the classification scheme as an unambiguous placement is not always possible.

For the classification of IT governance frameworks the set of characteristics is summed up in three different dimensions: (1) general framework attributes, (2) framework design and (3) framework application. The three dimensions are derived from the considerations by (Fettke et al., 2005; Walter and Krcmar, 2006; IT Governance Institute, 2006b; 2003; Schmidt, 2007) and their approaches for criteria for characterising process reference models.

General framework attributes (1) are used to describe the basic characteristics of an IT governance framework. The purpose of the selected attributes is to provide users as well as framework developers a first overview of the framework relating to its addressed GRC area, the targeted audience, origin of the framework, and the primary sources, where the framework is described in more detail. Comparable attributes also have been applied for reference models (Schmidt, 2007). In addition, and along with the classification scheme provided by the IT Governance Institute (IT Governance Institute, 2006b), further characteristics concerning the design and use of IT governance frameworks are provided (the list is not exhaustive).

For the *framework design* (2) attributes pertaining to the construction and organisation of the model such as the used concept of "IT governance" or the basic structure of the model are proposed. The intention here is to help potential users or framework developers to better understand the concepts behind an IT governance framework. For the *framework application* (3) differentiating attributes with respect to the deployment of the framework such as tool support or practicality of evidence are proposed. The identified attributes should help users in the selection of a proper framework as well as show developers possibilities for improvement of their framework.

Table 1 illustrates an exemplary application of the classification scheme by using the CobiT framework. A detailed description of the differentiating attributes is given in the following subsections. This template helps to map the attributes of the existing IT governance frameworks and the derived requirements within the healthcare to get a requirement overlap on which the IT GRC Framework for Healthcare will be based on.

Dimension	Attribute	Example
General framework attributes	Name	Control Objectives for Information and Related Technology
	Acronym	CobiT
	Current Version (year of publication)	4.1 (2007)
	Primary source	Information Systems Audit and Control Association (ISACA) and the IT Governance Institute (ITGI)
	Seconary source	www.itgi.org/cobit
	GRC area	Governance, Risk, Compliance
	Origin	Practice
	Targeted audience	Management-oriented
	Access	Freely available
	Domain	Public-domain
Framework design	Concept of IT governance	CobiT recognises 34 IT processes that are grouped into four domains. The four domains are: Plan and Organise, Acquire and Implement, Deliver and Support, Monitor and Evaluate.
	Composition	Each process has a level of maturity (numerical) from 0-5. (0 is non-existent and 5 is optimised.) This scale can be used for a number of key evaluations, such as the level of maturity a process is currently at within your organisation, what level of maturity the processes should be at, what level is considered best practice, & what level the best of your competitors/other organisations have achieved.
	Reliability	Validated & verified
	Mutability	Industry-neutral, mutable
Framework Application	Support	Textual description & tool support
	Practicality of evidence	Implicit improvement activities

Table 1: Example of a classified IT governance framework

4.1. Framework Design

The framework design attributes are used to describe the form and style of a framework. For this purpose, the attributes concept of IT governance, composition, reliability, and mutability are proposed. The attribute concept of IT governance answers the question how the topic of IT governance is approached and to which extent the examined frameworks address the different delimitations which have been discussed in the sections 3 and 4. As Spafford (2003) points out, there is limited overlap between the IT governance standards – most frameworks or best practices are reflected on an one-dimensional manner by the related literature, either focusing on (1) processes, i.e. how IT processes deliver the information that the business needs to achieve its objectives (IT Governance Institute, 2007), on (2) lifecycle, i.e. the way service management is structured, and the way the various lifecycle components are linked to each other and to the entire lifecycle system within the IT (Office of Government Commerce; 2005), or on (3) people capability, i.e. to which extent the management is able to create a mechanism through which it can provide the business with technology leadership (Calder, 2005). The concept of IT governance often motivates the composition of the framework. The attribute composition examines the aspect of the methodical approach applied within the frameworks (i.e. Six Sigma, balanced scorecard or maturity model approaches). Maturity models are increasingly being applied within the field of IT, both as informed approach for continuous improvement (Ahern et al., 2004) or as means of benchmarking or self-assessment (Conwell et al., 2000; Hakes, 1996). Conwell et al. (2000) distinguish three basic maturity model designs: (1) Maturity grids aim at illustrating a number of levels of maturity in a simple, textual manner (normally not exceeding a few pages of text), (2) Likert-like questionnaires are comparable with maturity grids, but the focus is more inclined on to scoring specific statements of "good practice" and not to describing the overall levels of maturity, and (3) CMM-like models, which are based upon a more formal architecture, specifying a number of goals and key practices to reach a predefined level of sophistication. Although more elaborate, CMM-like models also entail a greater complexity due to a wide range of scales and subscales for the assessment of maturity. Another important characteristic to enhance the reusability of an IT governance framework is its degree of reliability (Betz, 2007; Lee and Lee, 2009). Conwell et al. (2000) differentiate between verified and validated frameworks. Verification is thereby the process of determining that a framework "represents the developer's conceptual description and specifications with sufficient accuracy" and validation is the degree to which a framework is an "accurate representation of the real world from the perspective of the intended uses of the framework. If we examine the identified framework, it can be concluded that most of them cannot be categorised as validated (perhaps at most as verified). Thus, in order to enhance the reusability and reduce criticism on the poor theoretical grounding of IT governance frameworks in literature (Keyes-Pearce, 2002; Gottschalk, 2006; Calder, 2005) the emphasis on developing new IT governance frameworks should lay on extensively testing these models in terms of validity, reliability and generalisability.

The last characteristic concerning the design of the IT governance frameworks is the level of mutability. This is of particular importance – but for all that sometimes neglected – as, on the one hand, the business requirements are growing and therefore the framework's solutions stages and improvement activities have to be refaced from time to time (Krey et al., 2010) (e.g. modify requirements for reaching a certain maturity level due to the emergence of new best practices and technologies), on the other hand, changes in the form and function are needed to ensure the standardisation and industry acceptance of the framework (e.g. amend the framework focus areas to be compliant with changed organisational structures or legal restraints).

4.2. Framework Application

To describe the framework application, the attributes support of application and practicality of evidence are proposed. As regards the support of the model application, three stages of assistance are differentiated. In the first case, the users are given no supporting materials at all. Especially de facto standards tend to omit what the best starting point is and which methods should be use to achieve the objectives.

The more sophisticated frameworks, also deliver a textual description or handbook how to configure the deployment of the framework. However, the most advanced auxiliary means is the instantiation of the IT governance framework or parts of it on form of software tools (Johannsen et al., 2007). Another interesting characteristic concerning a framework for IT governance use is the practicality of evidence (i.e. the way how suggestions for improvement are made). In this regard, it is distinguished between implicit improvement activities, i.e. a general recommendation on the tacit assumption of the predefined objectives, and explicit recommendations, for example telling exactly what to do in order to enhance a particular activity, process or skill. In the case of the reviewed IT governance frameworks, a clear tendency to implicit recommendations exists. However, this is not astonishing given that the definition of explicit improvement activities is difficult or sometimes even futile. Nevertheless, explicit recommendations are desirable when a framework addresses a precisely delimited problem domain and the dissimilarity of the organisational realities does not play a major role.

5. Conclusion

Despite extensive research in the field of IT governance, considerable work is needed to further the understanding of IT governance, and to develop a successful holistic measure of IT governance. To enable IT governance to become an accepted part of organizational strategic and operational governance processes, it is important that researchers develop more practical methods for organizations to use in establishing and assessing IT governance (Johannsen et al., 2007; Lee and Lee, 2009). It is thus necessary to clarify the concept of IT governance through systematically classifying and drawing together various definitions so far offered.

The conduct of future research addressing the issues raised in the prior sections should lead to improved IT governance within each GRC area and the establishment of holistic frameworks of IT governance. A number of researchers including van Grembergen (2004) and Peterson (2004) have attempted to develop holistic IT governance frameworks but there is still much room for improvement in fusing IT governance into one process. New work could then specify its theoretical framework and begin to offer operative guidelines to hospital practitioners, for example, through suggesting some of the practical implications of different IT governance designs. To make sure that the corporate hospital strategy leads to adequate business decisions a Healthcare IT Governance Framework will be needed. This framework can help to minimize risks and should consider the special requirements of the health care sector.

Therefore, the classification of the frameworks in the field of IT governance was the first step in the evaluation of different frameworks. As Thomas (2005) noted, a framework developer "orients his decision on the use of a reference model only on whether he can recognize a potential benefit from the model. In order to make this decision the reference model must be made available to the user."

6. References

Addy, Rob, ed. *Effective IT Service Management: To ITIL and Beyond!* Berlin, Heidelberg: Springer-Verlag Berlin Heidelberg, 2007. http://dx.doi.org/10.1007/978-3-540-73198-6 / http://www.dandelon.com/intelligentSEARCH.nsf/alldocs/3274F6B5C35858C1C12572DC00 1A3305/.

Ahern, D. M., A. Clouse, and R. Turner, eds. *CMMI distilled: A practical introduction to integrated process improvement.* Bosten: Addison Wesley, 2004.

Betz, Charles T. *Architecture and patterns for IT service management, resource planning, and governance: Making shoes for the cobbler's children.* Amsterdam: Morgan Kaufmann/Elsevier, 2007. http://www.gbv.de/dms/hbz/toc/ht014953145.pdf.

Calder, Alan, ed. *It Governance: Guidelines for Directors*: IT Governance Publishing, 2005.

Cilli, C., ed. *IT governance: Why a guideline?* Information Systems Control Journal, vol. 3, p. 22-24, 2003. http://www.itgi.org/Template.cfm?Section=Home&CONTENTID=35752&TEMPLATE=/ContentManagement/ContentDisplay.cfm, accessed May 2010.

Conwell, C. L., R. Enright, and M. A. Stutzman, eds. *Capability maturity models support of modeling and simulation verification, validation, and accreditation: Winter Simulation Conference 2000.* San Diego, USA, 2000.

Fettke, Peter, Loos, Peter, and Zwicker, Jörg. "Business Process Reference Models: Survey and Classification." In *Workshop on Business Process Reference Models,* edited by Christoph Bussler and Armin Haller. Nancy, France, 2005.

Goeken, Matthias, and Stefanie Alter, eds. *IT Governance Frameworks as Methods: Proceedings of the 10th International Conference on Enterprise Information Systems, ICEIS 2008, 12 - 16, June.* Barcelona, Spain, 2008.

Gottschalk, Peter, ed. *E-business strategy, sourcing, and governance.* Hershey PA: Idea Group Pub., 2006.

Guldentops, Erik, Gary Hardy, Jimmy Gary Heschl, and Sharon Taylor, eds. *Aligning Cobit, ITIL and ISO 17799 for Business Benefit: A Management Briefing from ITGI und OGC.* www.itil.co.uk/includes/ITIL-COBiT.pdf, accessed May 2010.

Hakes, C., ed. *The corporate self assessment handbook.* London: Chapman and Hall, 1996.

Heier, Hauke, Hans P. Borgman, and Mervyn G. Maistry, eds. *Examining the relationship between IT governance software and business value of IT: Evidence from four case studies: Proceedings of the 40th Hawaii International Conference on System Sciences.* Hawaii, 2007.

ISACA Switzerland Chapter, ed. *CoP, Cobit, Marion, IT-Grundschutzhandbuch: vier Methoden im Vergleich,* 1998. http://www.isaca.ch/files/DO6_Arbeitsgruppen/igcop_broschuere.pdf.

Johannsen, Wolfgang, Goeken, Matthias, Just, Daniel, and Tami, Farsin. *Referenzmodelle für IT-Governance: Strategische Effektivität und Effizienz mit COBIT, ITIL & Co.* 1st ed. Heidelberg: dpunkt-Verl., 2007. http://deposit.d-nb.de/cgi-bin/dokserv?id=2838359&prov=M&dok_var=1&dok_ext=htm.

Johnstone, D., S. L. Huff, and B. Hope, eds. *IT projects: Conclict, governanace and systems thinking*. Proceeding on the 39th Hawaii International Conference on System Sciences, 2006.

Jordan, Ernie, and Silcock, Luke. *Beating IT risks*. Chichester: J. Wiley, 2005. http://www.gbv.de/dms/hbz/toc/ht014249257.pdf.

Keyes-Pearce, Susan. "Rethinking the Importance of IT Governance in the e-World." In *Proceedings of the 6th Pacific Asia Conference on Information Systems PACIS-2002*. Tokyo, 2002.

Krey, Mike, Bettina Harriehausen, Matthias Knoll, and Steven Furnell, eds. *IT Governance and its spread in Swiss Hospitals: Proceedings of the IADIS International Conference e-Health 2010*. Freiburg, 2010.

Lahti, Christian, and Roderick Peterson, eds. *Sarbanes-Oxley Compliance Using COBIT and Open Source Tools*: Syngress, 2005.

Lee, Junghoon, and Lee, Changjin. "IT Governance - Based IT strategy and Management: Literature Review and Future Reserach Directrions." In *Information technology governance and service management: Frameworks and adaptations*, edited by Aileen Cater-Steel. Hershey: Information Science Reference [u.a.], 2009.

Menzies, Christof, ed. *Sarbanes-Oxley und Corporate Compliance: Nachhaltigkeit, Optimierung, Integration*. Stuttgart: Schäffer-Poeschel, 2006. http://deposit.ddb.de/cgi-bin/dokserv?id=2749173&prov=M&dok_var=1&dok_ext=htm / http://www.gbv.de/dms/bsz/toc/bsz250745674inh.pdf.

Office of Government Commerce, ed. *Service delivery: ITIL The key to managing IT services*. 9th ed. London: TSO (The Stationery Office), 2005.

Peterson, Ryan R., ed. *Exploring the impact of electronic business readiness on leadership capabilities in information technology governance: In Proceedings of the 35th Hawaii International Conference on System Sciences*, 2003.

Schmidt, Andreas, ed. *State of the Art des IT-Service Managements*. GRIN Verlag, 2007.

Sohal, A. S., and P. Fitzpatrick, eds. *IT governance and management in large Australian organizations.*, 2002.

Spafford, George, ed. *The Benefits of Standard IT Governance Frameworks*, 2003. http://www.itmanagementonline.com/Resources/Articles/The_Benefits_of_Standard_IT_Governance_Frameworks.pdf, accessed June 2010.

Standards Australia, ed. *AS 8015-2005: Corporate governance of information and communication technology*, 2005. http://standards.com.au, accessed May 2010.

van Grembergen, Wim, ed. *Introduction to the minitrack: IT governanace ants its mechnisms: Proceedings of the 35th Hawaii International Conference on System Sciences (HICSS)*, 2002.

van Grembergen, Wim, ed. *Strategies for information technology governance*. Hershey, Pa., London: Idea Group Publishing, 2004. http://www.gbv.de/dms/hbz/toc/ht013914680.pdf.

van Grembergen, Wim, and de Haes, Steven. *Implementing information technology governance: Models, practices, and cases*. Hershey, Pa.: IGI Publ., 2008. http://www.gbv.de/dms/hbz/toc/ht015362476.pdf.

Walter, S., and H. Krcmar, eds. *Reorganisation der IT-Prozesse auf Basis von Referenzmodellen: Eine kritische Analyse*. it-Service-Management, Heft 2, 2006.

Weill, Peter, and Jeanne W. Ross, eds. *IT governance: How top performers manage IT decision rights for superior results*. Boston, Mass.: Harvard Business School Press, 2007. http://www.gbv.de/dms/bowker/toc/9781591392538.pdf

University of Plymouth, UK, 24-28 November, 2010

Agile Limitations and Model-Driven Opportunities for Software Development Projects

K.Mairon[1,2], M.Buchheit[2], M.Knahl[2], S.Atkinson[1], S.M.Furnell[1] and U.Schreier[2]

[1]Centre for Security, Communications and Network Research,
University of Plymouth, Plymouth, United Kingdom
[2]Furtwangen Research Node, Faculty of Business Information Systems
Hochschule Furtwangen University, Germany
e-mail: klaus.mairon@hs-furtwangen.de

Abstract

The development of business applications has become increasingly complex and cost-sensitive. Thus discussions about the appropriate software development process model and the possibility to increase efficiency are frequent. This paper summarizes the limitations of agile process models and analyses how the limitations can be overcome through the concepts of the Model-Driven Software Development. Finally there is an outlook to the further research with the intention to combine agile and model-driven concepts.

Keywords

Agile Software Development, Software Development Process Model, Model-Driven Software Development

1. Introduction

Today the development of business applications is influenced by increased project complexity, shortened development cycles and high expectations in quality (Baskerville & Pries-Heje, 2004). Rising costs in the software development are an additional motivation to improve the productivity by the choice of a suitable development process (Jones, 2008).

In the development of complex applications models are of great importance. Models reduce complexity by abstraction. Additionally models offer the possibility to build different views onto an application. If models are sufficiently formal they are suitable for the automated transformation into source code. For this reason an important acceleration and quality factor in the software development is attributed to the Model-Driven Software Development (Stahl and Völter, 2005). On the other hand Model-Driven Software Development requires quite high initial work for the definition of meta-models, domain-specific languages and transformation rules for the code generation process.

A different approach to improve productivity is the use of agile process models like Scrum, Extreme Programming (XP) or Feature Driven Development (FDD) (Lindval et al. 2004). For these process models an early production of source code and the

43

adjustment of executable partial results are important aspects of the process. The communication with the end user and the direct feedback are the most important success factors for a project and facilitate quick reactions on requirement changes (Eckstein, 2010). In agile methods modelling often plays a subordinated role. The requirements will be documented via "user stories" (XP) or "features" (Scrum, FDD). They are summarized either in Product- or Sprint-Backlogs (Scrum)(Cohn, 2005) or in Feature-Sets (FDD) (Coad *et al.* 1999). This doesn't mean that there is no documentation or modelling in the development process. But only FDD describes modelling as an explicit step in the development process.

In the development of large and in many cases complex business applications it is common practice to use more formal process models with strong administrative aspects, such as for example the Rational Unified Process (RUP) or the V-model. However, Eckstein describes in (Eckstein, 2004) that agile process models can be used in large projects instead of the heavyweight process models. This raises the question to what extend the usage of models and the Model-Driven Software Development can be integrated into the agile development process. In the heavyweight software development processes like RUP modelling is a substantial part of the process and the technique of the Model-Driven Software Development may be integrated into these processes well. But in the less formal process models like Scrum there is no specified approach to integrate Model-driven Software Development. Another challenge is if the development team is distributed to various locations.

The paper will discuss the limitations of agile process models and how Model-Driven Software Development can assist these processes to get a successful high-quality and maintainable overall result. Based on three weaknesses of agile process models is shown how these can be mitigated by typical MDSD-technologies (e.g. through the use of domain-specific languages, or refactoring at the architecture level). For this, the paper will outline the first approaches and further steps of a corresponding research project.

2. Limitations of Agile Development Processes

In (Ramesh *et al.* 2006) some challenges for the application of agile development processes in large (especially distributed) teams were identified. As an example there is the conflict between communication need and communication independence. Agile development processes are based on informational communication rather than detailed documentation. But in large projects with many team members there is a need for formal methods such as detailed specifications or architectural design to give the developers the information needed. Also in (Turk *et al.* 2002) the importance of face-to-face communication in projects is indicated as a limitation of agile processes for distributed teams.

In (Turk *et al.* 2002) the authors explain several limitations for agile processes. These are amongst others:

- No or limited/poor support for distributed development.
- No process support to identify reusable software components.
- Problems in refactoring large and complex software systems.

In the following these points are clarified.

2.1. Agile principles in distributed development projects

The so-called agile principles (Agile Alliance, 2001b) underpin the value system of the Agile Manifesto (Agile Alliance, 2001a). They give guidance on the implementation of an agile approach. However, principles such as "continuous delivery of valuable software" lead to a variety of challenges for distributed projects.

Therefore, the early and continuous delivery of software requires a stronger collaboration between all locations as in non-distributed projects. To build a software release across different geographic locations is more difficult than if the team members would sit together. The challenge is, not to accomplish several individual systems on the various sites but one coherent system.

Furthermore, it is very difficult to achieve a close cooperation between business people and developers. In addition to the spatial distance there are often also cultural differences, and large differences in time zones can complicate the cooperation further. Nevertheless, all project members must get a common understanding of the business requirements. In (Eckstein, 2010), the author describes different roles (e.g. the "traveller") to enhance the communication and collaboration in distributed projects.

2.2. Problems creating reusable software components

In agile processes the focus is on the development in short cycles and an early delivery of valuable software. This precludes developing generalized solutions (Turk et al 2005). But it is clear that reusability could yield long-term benefits. According to (Turk et al. 2002) the development of reusable software components or generalized solutions is best assigned in teams that are primarily engaged in the development of reusable artifacts.

(Turk et al. 2002) refers to a study (Basili and Rombach, 1991), after which it is best to separate the product development from the development of reusable software components. The development of reusable software components requires a special attention to the quality, because errors in these components are often of greater relevance. In fact it is desirable to develop reusable components in a timely manner, but after (Turk et al. 2002) it is not clear how agile methods can be adapted accordingly. A possible solution to this problem is discussed by (Hummel and Atkinson, 2007). The authors propose to integrate the identification of reusable components tightly to the test-driven development cycles.

2.3. Problems in refactoring large systems

Agile methods are based on the premise that good design is achieved through constant refactoring (Fowler, 1999). This cannot be sustained in large complex systems. The increasing dependencies between software components make the code refactoring over the entire application costly. At the same time it increases the risk of errors. (Turk *et al.* 2002) also refers to software in which functionality is so closely coupled and integrated that it isn't possible to develop the software incrementally. In these cases can also be developed iteratively, but the code parts that are created within an iteration will always be incomplete.

In agile projects Test Driven Development (TDD) is a well-proven method to reduce the risk of errors during the refactoring process. But, with the increasing complexity and the growing number of dependencies between components the effort for the maintenance of test cases increases too. Incomplete code parts will complicate this additionally.

3. Agility and Model-Driven Development

In below it is to be shown how it is possible to support the agile principles with Model-Driven Software Development (MDSD).

- *"Our highest priority is to satisfy the customer through early and continuous delivery of valuable software."* The Model-Driven Software Development starts with the definition of the domain architecture and the derivation of the transformation rules. This means a certain lead-time before a first executable result can be delivered. However, (Stahl & Völter, 2005) recommend deriving the domain architecture from a prototype or a reference implementation. This prototype can be used as a first delivery to the customer and is already providing valuable feedback for further development. If the prototype is developed incrementally, the project will get feedback continuously, and the architects can develop the domain-architecture in parallel.

- *"Business people and developers must work together daily throughout the project."* The close cooperation between business people and developers can become more intensive by the modelling. When using a domain-specific language (DSL) this is still more strongly accentuated. Mistakes can be detected more quickly because the developer and the domain expert are talking at the same abstraction level. In (Ambler, 2002) the author argues that the communication between developers and business people is the primary reason for modelling and emphasizes the advantages of the model as a basis for reviews and feedback sessions.

- *"Continuous attention to technical excellence and good design enhances agility."* A frequent criticism at the Model-Driven Software Development is that the developers have less freedom for their own choices in the development of the software. On the other hand high quality is guaranteed by the automated transformation from models into code and the standardized implementation (Stahl & Völter, 2005).

- *"Working software is the primary measure of progress."* As explained in (Stahl & Völter, 2005) the creation of executable software can be accelerated significantly, because of recurring tasks that are automated. The developers can focus on the implementation of business logic.

In addition, the MDSD helps to mitigate the limitations of agile software development processes.

3.1. Reusing domain artefacts

In the context of Model-Driven Software Development two aspects must be considered to support building reusable software components: the domain-architecture and the development of business logic.

In addition to the application architecture the domain architecture is an important artefact of the Model-Driven Software Development. According to (Stahl & Völter, 2005) the domain architecture is defined as the aggregation of the meta-model of a domain and a platform with the corresponding transformations and tools. The domain architecture defines the concepts that will be formally supported in the model and how those are mapped on the given platform.

The development of the domain architecture should be implemented in parallel to the application development. An essential part is the reference implementation from which the transformation-rules are derived. The reference implementation has a much higher relevance as a conventional prototype. Together with the reference model or reference design, it demonstrates the application and implementation of the domain modelling language.

The domain-architecture itself is a reuse of architectural elements. The development of the DSL and the derivation of the relevant transformation-rules assist the identification of reusable components and modules.

During the application development, the modelling may help the developer to focus on the business logic and the semantics. Because of the higher abstraction level it is easier to identify reusable business components.

3.2. Refactoring at an higher level (architectural refactoring)

Support for refactoring is one of the strengths of Model-Driven Software Development. Refactoring can be applied to models, platforms, transformation rules and the implemented code. Thus the Model-Driven Software Development facilitates the reaction to changes clearly.

Changes in business requirements can be adopted through the generation process very quickly and in a consistent way. For example: additional attributes in business classes can automatically be reflected in the user interface, in the database definition, and in all relevant data structures. Only the adaptation of the affected business logic has to be done via source code refactoring. This is the most common type of refactoring and is needed whenever new requirements affect existing code.

But another kind of changed requirements is significantly more complex to manage. These are changed technical requirements like adjustments of the architecture or the replacement of an underlying technical framework. In the model-driven approach, architectural changes can be performed at a central point: at the templates and the transformation rules. These changes are taking over for the whole application automatically.

3.3. Supporting agile and distributed projects

In the context of distributed development, it is difficult to decide what should be developed at what location. This is also in an agile project. Additionally there is the question of how to achieve a common understanding of the future application.

Section 3.1. describes the need of developing additional artefacts in the context of Model-Driven Software Development. But the creation of the domain architecture can be separated well from the development of the business logic and can be developed by a team located at a remote location without direct customer contact. At the same time the development of the reference implementation, the description of the reference design and associated programming model contributes to the general understanding of the application architecture.

(Ambler, 2004) argues that the quality of the requirements descriptions is enhanced with a domain specific modelling language. This applies to all teams in a distributed project environment that operate close to the customer. However, the additional abstraction by the domain specific modelling language is well suited to help all project members to get the required overall picture of the application.

(Eckstein, 2004) describes how agile approaches can be applied in large projects. On this basis, she describes in (Eckstein, 2010) the use of agile methods for distributed teams. According to the author, just the emphasis on communication in agile approaches is the essential advantage for working in large and distributed teams. The challenge for such projects is to achieve a common vision of the target system and mutual trust. While the usage of a domain specific modelling language supports the communication, the reference design and reference implementation provides transparency. This enables the team to reach this goal.

In this way, the Model-Driven Software Development can improve the limited support of agile methods for distributed development projects.

4. Conclusions and further research

According to (Parsons et al. 2007), almost 40% of the surveyed IT professionals use one or more agile methods in software development. Close cooperation with the customer and refactoring are commonly referred to as the agile techniques with the greatest benefit in terms of quality, productivity and satisfaction.

The close cooperation with the customer may be supported additionally through the Model-Driven Software Development and the use of domain-specific languages. The use of a common modelling language supports obtaining a shared vision of the software that has to be developed.

The agile technique of refactoring assists the continuous improvement and development towards the target architecture. The Model-Driven Software Development supports this effect and brings additional efficiency into the development. The code generation is also a guarantor for a unified and reproducible implementation and high quality. The Model-Driven Software Development can help to scale the agile techniques through the explicit separation of the development of the domain architecture and the application development.

The further research will be focused on the following aspects. First, the issue is examined what kind of modelling is suitable to enhance the communication with the users, without creating unnecessary formalism. For this, approaches for agile model-driven development are considered, as described in (Ambler, 2004). Additional information provides a case study of the Rey Juan Carlos University in Madrid, which took account of these approaches in their framework MIDAS (Cáceres *et al.* 2004). An agile process should be defined, that optimally integrates the modelling and provides the information sufficient for the model-driven development.

Another aspect attends to the process of the model-driven development and the relevant artefacts (e.g. the domain architecture). The goal is to define an agile process for the development of these artefacts. For this, best practice experiences in model-driven development like in (Baker *et al.* 2005) will be analyzed. In addition, a survey about the usage of MDSD as well as the adaptation of agile process models in practice will be done to get additional information about industrial experiences. For this primarily the German IT-market will be examined, which has suffered recently from particularly high and rising costs.

It is the intention to define and develop a framework to facilitate agile and model-driven software engineering. This includes essential procedures, methods and tools. The framework can be applied to the development, testing, operation or project management. It is envisaged that the main focus will be the adoption of the framework to combine agile and model-driven development and to derive a new software development process. The framework will be applied to a software development project to evaluate its usability and effectiveness.

5. References

Agile Alliance (2001a), „Manifesto for Agile Software Development", www.agilealliance.org (Accessed 15 July 2010)

Agile Alliance (2001b), „Principles behind the Agile Manifesto", www.agilealliance.org/principles.html (Accessed 15 July 2010)

Ambler, S. (2002), *Agile Modeling. Effective Practices for eXtreme Programming and the Unified Process*, New York: John Wiley & Sons, ISBN: 0-471-20282-7.

Ambler, S. (2004), *The Object Primer, 3rd Edition. Agile Model-Driven Development with UML 2.0*, New York: Cambridge University Press, ISBN: 978-0-521-54018-6.

Baker, P., Loh, S. & Weil, F. (2005), „Model-Driven Engineering in a Large Industrial Context - Motorola Case Study", in: *Lecture Notes in Computer-Science. Model Driven Engineering Languages and Systems.*, 3713, pp. 476-491.

Baskerville, R. & Pries-Heje, J. (2004) „Short cycle time systems development", in: *Information Systems Journal*, 14 (3), pp. 237-264.

Basili, V.R. and Rombach, H.D. (1991), "Support for comprehensive reuse", in: *Software Engineering Journal*. 6 (5), pp. 303-316.

Cáceres, P., Díaz, F. & Marcos, E. (2004) „Integrating an Agile Process in a Model Driven Architecture", in *GI Jahrestagung 2004*. pp. 265-270.

Coad, P., Lefebvre, E. and DeLuca, E. (1999), *Java Modeling in Color with UML. Enterprise Components and Process*, Upper Saddle River: Prentice Hall International, ISBN: 978-0-130-11510-2.

Cohn, M. (2009), *Succeeding with Agile: Software Development using Scrum*, Amsterdam: Addison-Wesley Longman, ISBN: 978-0-321-57936-2.

Eckstein, J. (2004), *Agile Software Development in the Large - Diving Into the Deep*. New York: Dorset House, ISBN 978-0-932-63357-6.

Eckstein, J. (2010), *Agile Software Development with Distributed Teams: Staying Agile in a Global World*, New York: Dorset House, ISBN: 978-0-932-63371-2.

Fowler, M. (1999), *Refactoring: Improving the Design of Existing Code*. Amsterdam: Addison-Wesley Longman, ISBN: 978-0-201-48567-7

Hummel, O. and Atkinson, C. (2007), "Supporting Agile Reuse Through Extreme Harvesting", in: *Agile Processes in Software Engineering and Extreme Programming, 8th International Conference*. Como, Italy pp. 28-37.

Jones, C. (2008) *Applied Software Measurement: Global Analysis of Productivity and Quality* 3rd ed., New York: Mcgraw-Hill Professional, ISBN: 978-0-071-50244-3

Lindval, M., Muthig, D., Dagnino, A., Wallin, C., Kiefer, D., May, J. & Kähkönen, T. (2004) „Agile Software Development in Large Organizations", in: *Computer*, 37 (12), pp. 26-34.

Parsons, D., Ryu, H.R. & Lal, R. (2007), "The Impact of Methods and Techniques on Outcomes from Agile Software Development Projects". In *Organisational Dynamics of Technology-Based Innovation: Diversifying the Research Agenda.* pp. 235-249.

Ramesh, B., Cao, L., Mohan, K. and Xu, P. (2006), "Can distributed software development be agile?", *Communications of the ACM*, 49 (10), pp. 41-46.

Stahl, T. & Völter, M. (2005), *Model-Driven Software Development. Technology, Engineering, Management*, Chichester: John Wiley & Sons, ISBN: 0-470-02570-0.

Turk, D., France, R. & Rumpe, B. (2002), "Limitations of Agile Software Processes", in: *Third International Conference on eXtreme Programming and Agile Processes in Software Engineering.* Alghero, Italy, pp. 43-46.

Turk, D., France, R., Rumpe, B. (2005), "Assumptions Underlying Agile Software Development Processes", *Journal of Database Management.* 16 (4), pp. 62-87.

System Design for Embedded Automotive Systems

S.Vergata[1,2], J.Wietzke[1], A.Schütte[1] and P.S.Dowland[2]

[1]Faculty of Computer Science, University of Applied Sciences Darmstadt, Germany
[2]Centre for Security, Communications and Network Research,
University of Plymouth, United Kingdom
{s.vergata, j.wietzke, a.schuette}@fbi.h-da.de, p.dowland@plymouth.ac.uk

Abstract

These days, a modern car will be a complete office, lounge and chauffeur system, composed from different systems, that incorporate themselves into an on board automotive cluster system. This will behave like one component and offer a customized user interface. To facilitate the system development of such a cluster system, different system interfaces like memory and inter process communication mechanisms need to be provided through all the cooperating systems. Embedded systems are now facing the same problems, which occurred years ago in the server world. One of the major automotive original equipment manufacturers chose Intel's Atom CPU as the target platform for their latest development. This step shows that a modern x86 based architecture could provide the basis for a reliable automotive system. There is now an opportunity to introduce virtual machine (VM) technology combined with new security and reliability methods in the embedded automotive sector.

Keywords

Embedded systems, Hypervisor architecture, Automotive systems, Scheduler, Security compartments

1. Introduction

In the automotive business, the software development is domain oriented. Telephone, speech recognition and speech output, for example, were running on their own processor in the last generation. Only because of cost reasons and higher HW-integration, many domains nowadays get combined on the same processor. We count between 8 and 16 domains, some of them supplied by third party vendors, often directly contracted by the OEM.

It is no surprise, that they follow their own priority scheme and scheduling according to their own history. At the same time ideas like domain based binary delivery, get promoted which represent a domain each, contributors are requested to deliver their code as a binary, ready to run, with APIs specified and followed, but without priority and scheduling coordinated.

Caused by the chosen Round Robin scheduling in the OS for the moment, this approach forces all provided binaries to use one common priority (10), which is not a valid concept for a product, causing a high complexity in integrating all components together in one single system. A new type of system architecture has to be introduced which separates system critical and resource hungry applications case by case.

A recent found automotive alliance named GENIVI selected the OpenSource project MeeGo (Hoffmann 2010) for their base system opening up the automotive sector for freely developed application, with all different types of system usage and requirements. The kernel 2.6.33 used in MeeGo uses a Completely Fair Scheduler (CFS) designed for an interactive desktop system. This scheduler evenly distributes available calculation time to all available threads (Jones 2009).

2. Problem Statement

One of the major operating systems for embedded automotive systems QNX, (Turley 2005), developed a new scheduler called Advanced Partition Scheduler (APS) to face the problem of partitioning CPU and resources in a complex software system for multiple application providers.

The current APS (Danko 2007) is tailored to a use-case perspective, in which high priority threads are collected into one partition, less important threads into another partition and so forth.

2.1. Budgeting

In this approach, budget inheritance is mandatory through use cases, which is not followed in all aspects.

There is an upcoming need for domain virtualization, in which each domain has its own sandbox with independent priorities and schemes. On this level, there is no need for a full virtualisation with different operating systems in different partitions. There is also no need for budgeting.

2.2. Concurrency of priorities

APS doesn't allow independent, non-coordinated priorities and scheduling schemes in different partitions. A somehow special and at the same time typical example of the concurrency of priorities and budgets in APS can be observed in the telephone environment.

Handsfree telephony collects audio samples and processes them one sample at a time. This processing includes echo compensation and has to run on maximum load (100% CPU usage) and on high priority, since crackling, robot voices and mutes should be avoided.

The typical average CPU usage behaviour for this is 50 %. So a characteristic CPU load looks like:

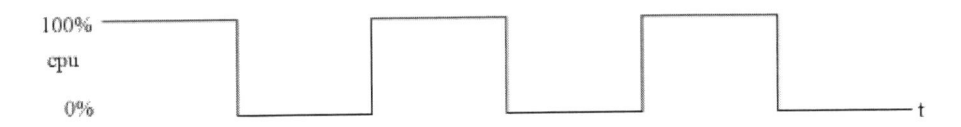

Figure 1 Typical CPU usage

In the same domain a so-called background thread is running which is allowed to use all remaining CPU power on a very low priority. If a mobile is connected the first time, all the SIM-card data will be downloaded to the automotive system. In our case, this thread fills up the idle gaps of this partition with its 50% load. So the averaged load in a given time slice will be at 75 %. The available APS Budget will be empty just before the high priority thread restart working. In a time window of 100 ms, perfect hands free will be achieved for 75 ms, the remaining 25 ms, the audio buffers will be empty, causing signal crackling or mutes.

2.3. Scheduling in critical mode

In this domain concepts, budgeting and priorities don't cope with each other. We will always face the combination of high and low priority threads in the same partition/domain, sometimes active, sometimes sleeping. Overspending budgets, like proposed and implemented in APS by declaring critical budgets is not a solution, since a thread in critical mode does not follow Round Robin anymore (Danko 2007).

3. Steps to a system design

The above described Problems show the need for a new type of system design in the embedded automotive sector. In the following sections two possible designs will be proposed.

3.1. Reduced clock scheduling

One solution could be a scheduling scheme, which distributes the CPU power in a fixed and fine granular scheme, so that it looks like we have e.g. 8 parallel processors, each hosting a partition. By that, they do not run on budgets but on reduced CPU clocks, each according to a given static configuration, predefined during system configuration time.

If a partition has threads neither running nor ready waiting, it can allow the scheduler to skip to the next partition. But this is the only dynamic aspect allowed.

A simple non-invasive implementation to gain experience could be the following: A 'Super'-thread on a high priority level next to kernel priority keeps a list of threads per partition. After booting, it starts to increase all threads of the first domain by a fixed value, so that they come first. For that the overall handled priority queues should be expanded by 64 up to 128, so that the addend will be 64 for raising up a domain to the according run level. The available add-on priority levels higher then 64 shouldn't be set by user threads but only by the 'Super'-thread.

Then the 'Super'-thread blocks on a timer with a sleeping time according to our granularity value (e.g. 1 ms). After waking up again, it sets the priorities of the first partition back to their normal value and increases all threads of the next partition.

The scheme specifying which domain follows which, is stored in a look up table. To ensure the configured timings for each domain, it is necessary to use a distributed pre-calculation based on the configured percentage each domain needs. Such a pre-calculation could be done by using a calculation scheme called Sainte-Laguë (Mueller 2003). This type of calculation is used for "seat distribution" in a government parliament.

A small example:

Let us assume a system specified by the following facts:

- 20 % CPU time reserved for base system

- 80% CPU time available slot time for distribution by Pre-Calc

Domain	D1	D2	D3	D4	D5
Percentage	35%	30%	20%	10%	5%
Slots	28	24	16	8	4

Table 1: Slot distribution per Domain

Table 1 shows that the overall available CPU slot time is distributed by the given percentage (division by 5 domains). D1 is the Domain with the highest configured percentage and with the highest calculated CPU-time-slots (28).

The smallest percentage step allowed should be 5%, so with a granularity of 5 each domain can allocate CPU time at configuration time. Smaller steps are possible but not reliable enough. The maximum number of domains should be 20, so it will be possible to distribute in a fair way and the overall system overhead for every scheduling step is small.

The scheduling algorithm could be similar to a Fair Share (Ferrer 2010) scheduling used in an OpenSource implementation called OpenVZ. This implementation also provides memory isolation, which could be useful for an implementation that can separate single domains and prevent them from interacting illegally with other domains.

By having separated domains with assured timeslots, everyone can run independently and use their assured maximum CPU time without interfering with other domain runtimes. On the overall system performance monitor a total system usage of $T_u = (100 - T_s) * T_d$ should be seen.

3.2. Virtualization

Virtualization began in the 1960s with IBM CP-40/67 and Cambridge Monitor System (CMS) (Parmelee 1972) as first type of hypervisor. The Patent granted to VMWare Inc. US006397242 (Devine 1998) opened up the x86 architecture for server virtualization. Virtualization on modern server systems does not only provide the possibility to use 100% computing power but also creates small containments easier to develop, maintain and rollout. To use the benefits achieved in x86- server virtualization an important step had to be taken, the switch over to x86 CPU.

One of the major automotive original equipment manufacturers chose Intel's Atom CPU as the target platform for their latest development (Otellini 2009). This step shows that a modern x86 based architecture could provide the basis for a reliable automotive system and in a second step opens up all the possibilities known from the server market to the automotive sector.

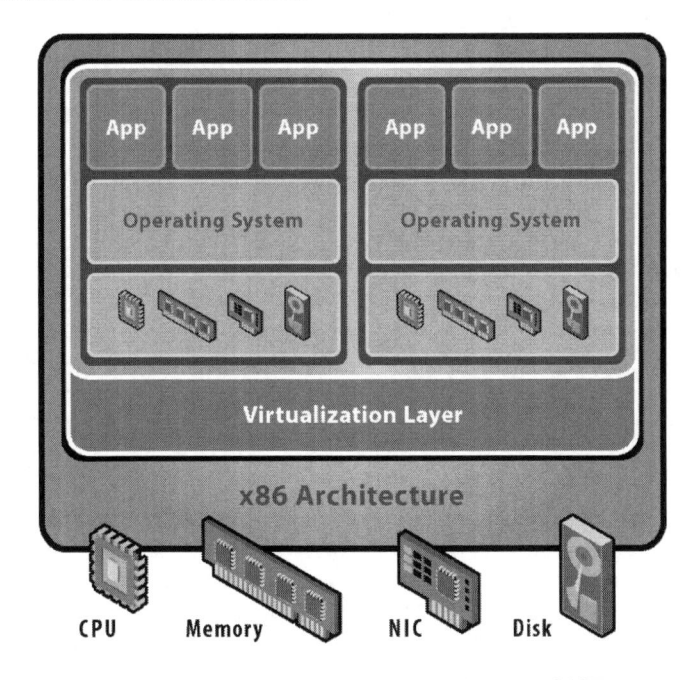

Figure 2: Virtualization Layer (VMware 2007)

As shown in Figure 2 the virtualization technique introduces an abstraction layer between the available hardware and the virtualized operating system. The CPU instructions get binary translated, replaced with hypercalls or mapped by the Virtualization Machine Monitor to a physical CPU. The chosen type of virtualization technique is dependent on the hardware. The figure below shows the different levels and the way a command travels through the layers.

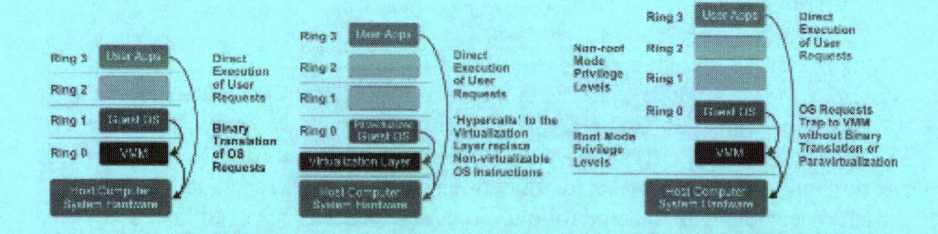

Figure 3: Different Types of Virtualization (VMware 2007)

Some work has been done taking virtualisation to the embedded market (VirtualLogix 2006). In the market existing virtualisation solutions separate into two virtualization types:

- System / Full virtualization

- Software / Container virtualization

In a full virtualization each running client has its own operating system and all the needed libraries. This creates a well-known system for the client and provides freedom for the developer. On the other hand it requires more CPU and memory, caused by multiple running OS-Kernels, an overhead on the system stack, and the separation of hardware resources.

To provide the possibility to run under the primary system kernel and by that to reduce the system overhead, a software virtualisation is needed. This has to provide secured execution compartments, memory abstraction and runtime control. Applications and used libraries run in this container and will be provided by the application programmer.

Both types of virtualizations have the possibility to provide a central debug instance to monitor and intercept applications, trace system calls or analyse memory allocation without modification in the running applications. With that centralized monitor, the integrator for the primary system has all methods available needs to check and control the single clients from outside without interfering into the provided system.

First evaluations and tests showed that not only a single virtualisation method is needed, moreover a multilevel virtualisation should be considered

The different types of virtualisation should be combined in one overall virtualisation solution to support all software components that may be required in a future system. The system virtualization requires hardware capable of providing the hardware-based virtualization extension. More and more CPUs introduced into the embedded market like the ARM Cortex A9 MPCore, Hitachi SH7789 or Intel Atom Z5xx are equipped with multiple independent core or virtualization extensions like Intels VT-x or AMD-V, providing the capabilities of a good performing virtualization technologies.

4. Conclusion and Outlook

Caused by the increasing amount of applications wanted in the automotive environment many problems will have to be faced in the future. Each application could have a varying way of development strategy, including scheduling, memory usage and much more. In this paper some insufficiencies could be identified, caused by integrating different complex software system together in one automotive system. Our proposals combine applications of different types in a non-interfering way together into one embedded system.

In the next steps of research, both proposals will be integrated into an overall system to provide full virtualization, software virtualization and reduced clock scheduling in secured compartments. With these three different types of systems containment it should be possible to integrate a variety of applications in one embedded system without interfering with each other. A complete system image could be loaded in a full virtualization environment. Reduced software systems without Kernel could be run in a container virtualization and hardware drivers or base applications could be run in a reduced clock scheduling.

The approach described in this paper separates all systems and assures the non-interfering between the systems. The design and realisation of a good performing communication method for the inter-system communications has to be considered in a next research milestone. In future research a new system design for embedded automotive systems will be developed considering security, efficiency and communication of different interacting software components.

5. References

Broy, M. (2006), *"Challenges in automotive software engineering"*, In: Proceedings of the 28th International Conference on Software Engineering, p. 33–42, ACM.

Chaudhary V., Cha M., Walters J., Guercio S., and Gallo S.. (2008) *"A comparison of virtualization technologies for hpc"*. In Advanced Information Networking and Applications,. AINA 2008. 22nd International Conference on, pages 861–868

Danko A. (2007), *"Adaptive Partitioning - Scheduler"*, http://community.qnx.com/sf/wiki/do/viewPage/projects.core_os/wiki/Adaptive_Partitioning_Scheduler (last accessed 06-Apr-2010)

Devine S., Bugnion E., and Rosenblum M. (1998), *"Virtualization system including a virtual machine monitor for a computer with a segmented architecture"*. US Patent #6,397,242.

Elkaduwe D. and Derrin P. and Elphinstone K. (2008), *"Kernel Design for Isolation and Assurance of Physical Memory"*, In: 1st Workshop on Isolation and Integration in Embedded Systems p. 35-40, ACM.

Ferrer R. (2010) *"Fair-share scheduling"*, http://wiki.openvz.org/Fair-share_scheduling (last accessed 10-Aug-2010)

Hoffmann J. (2010), *"What does GENIVI's selection of MeeGo mean?"*, http://meego.com/community/blogs/jahoffmann/2010/what-does-genivi's-selection-meego-mean, (last accessed 16-Aug-2010)

Jones M. T. (2009), *"Inside the linux 2.6 completely fair scheduler"*, http://www.ibm.com/developerworks/linux/library/l-completely-fair-scheduler/, (last accessed 20-Dec-2010).

Matthews J. N., Hu W., Hapuarachchi M., Deshane T., Dimatos D., Hamilton G., McCabe M., and Owens J.. *"Quantifying the performance isolation properties of virtualization systems"* In ExpCS '07: Proceedings of the 2007 workshop on Experimental computer science, page 6, New York, NY, USA, 2007. ACM.

Mueller D. C. (2003), *"Public Choice III"*, Cambridge University Press, pages 267-274

OpenICM (2010), Webpage of the OpenICM Framework, h-da - University of Applied Sciences Darmstadt, Germany, http://openicm.fbi.h-da.de (last accessed 20-Aug-2010).

Otellini P. (2009), *"Intel Developer Forum San Francisco Opening Keynote"*, http://download.intel.com/pressroom/kits/events/idffall_2009/pdfs/Otellini_IDF_transcript.pdf , (last accessed 01-Aug-2010)

Parmelee R. P., Peterson T. I., Tillman C. C., and Hatfield. D. J. *"Virtual storage and virtual machine concepts"*. IBM Systems Journal, 11(2):99 –130, 1972.

Pretschner, A., Broy, M., Kruger, IH. and Thomas S. (2007), *"Software engineering for automotive systems: A roadmap"*, In: International Conference on Software Engineering 2007, p. 55-71, IEEE.

Seelam S. R., Teller P.J. (2007), *"Virtual I/O scheduler: a scheduler of schedulers for performance virtualization"*, In: Proceedings of the 3rd international conference on Virtual execution environments, p. 105-115, ACM

Sangiovanni-Vincentelli, A. and Di Natale, M. (2007), *"Embedded System Design for Automotive Applications"*, In: Computer, volume 40, issue 10, p. 42–51, IEEE.

Turley J.(2005), *"Embedded systems survey: Operating systems up for grabs"*, http://www.eetimes.com/discussion/other/4025539/Embedded-systems-survey-Operating-systems-up-for-grabs (last accessed 18-Aug-2010)

VirtualLogix (2006), *"Meeting the Challenges of Connected Device Design Through Real-Time Virtualization"*, http://www.virtuallogix.com

VMware (2007), *"Understanding Full Virtualization, Paravirtualization, and Hardware Assist"*, http://www.vmware.com/resources/techresources/1008 (last accessed 10-Aug-2010)

Wietzke, J. and Tran, MT. (2005), *"Automotive Embedded Systeme"*, Xpert.press, Springer.

Integration of Model-Based Functional Testing Procedures within a Creation Environment for Value Added Services

P.Wacht[1,2], A.Lehmann[1,2], T.Eichelmann[1,2], W.Fuhrmann[3], U.Trick[1] and B.V.Ghita[2]

[1]Research Group for Telecommunication Networks, University of Applied Sciences Frankfurt/M., Frankfurt/M., Germany
[2]Centre for Security, Communications and Network Research, University of Plymouth, Plymouth, United Kingdom
[3]University of Applied Sciences Darmstadt, Darmstadt, Germany
e-mail: wacht@e-technik.org

Abstract

Actual Service Creation Environments (SCE) do not support functional testing of automatically created value added services. This leads to a problem as there is no verification that the service is created properly according to the requirement's specification. This paper presents an approach to integrate a testing framework into an existing SCE, which enables systematic and effective functional testing of value added services. The procedure is based on the idea that a behaviour model is created from which the amount of test cases for a specific service can be derived. The identified test cases are transferred to TTCN-3 (Testing and Test Control Notation 3) code and executed on the created service, which is the SUT (System under Test).

Keywords

SCE (Service Creation Environment); finite state machines; functional test automation; TTCN-3 (Testing and Test Control Notation 3)

1. Introduction

In the near future, network operators and service providers aim for Service Creation Environments (SCE) that enable fast, easy and cost efficient provisioning of value added services. Currently, the building of such SCEs has been done in several research projects, as in the TeamCom project (TeamCom, 2009; Lehmann et al., 2009). The TeamCom SCE offers a possibility for developers to design value added services with the help of a graphical user interface and the executable language BPEL (Business Process Execution Language). After the design is fulfilled it is analysed by a code generator and translated into the specific service code. Subsequently, the service can be deployed on an Application Server.

The TeamCom approach proved to work properly for several services. However, a very important aspect is not yet supported by the SCE: the integration of automated functional tests to validate and verify the created value added services. This enhancement of the SCE will have to be done, because functional tests are derived from the service's specification, which contains the customer's requirements and wishes for the service. So the integration of testing procedures enables a service provider to check if the built service meets the demands of a customer.

The aim of this paper is to show how testing procedures can be integrated within SCEs systematically. For this purpose, the ComGeneration (ComGeneration, 2010) project has been established that should provide a consistent solution to support the life cycle of a service by simplifying development, testing and provisioning of multimedia communication services. This approach reduces the expenditure of time and cost.

A similar approach to ComGeneration was accomplished in the project TT-Medal (TT-Medal, 2010), which has proven the advantages of using UML to generate TTCN-3 tests. Also, the firm Conformiq (Conformiq, 2010) implemented a test suite (Conformiq Tool Suite) which automates the design of functional tests for software and systems. However, the handling of the suite requires deep knowledge in UML and in several programming languages.

The content of this paper is structured as follows: In section 2 the consistent concept of the service and test platform is described. The 3rd section is concerned with the actual approach to describe customer's requirements within a "Service Description". Section 4 describes the relevant parts of the "Test Development" process and in section 5 the execution of test cases is introduced. Finally, section 6 offers a conclusion.

2. Service Creation and Testing Environment

Before looking at the detailed issues about how functional testing of value added services looks like, it is worthwhile having a look at the concept of the ComGeneration approach. Figure 1 gives an abstract overview.

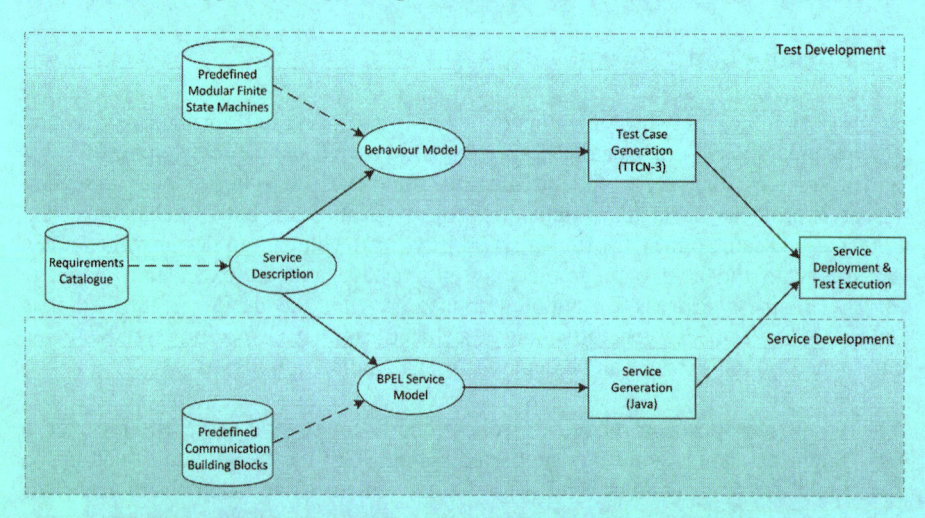

Figure 1: Service and test development for value added services

The shown architecture can be divided into two main layers: The Service Development and the Test Development. In between there are tasks that are relevant to both layers. The kinds of shapes illustrated in the picture have a special meaning, for instance, the container-like shapes generally represent predefined data which a person being involved in the process can choose from. This is shown by the dashed arrow in Figure 1. The circle shapes define actions where a human has to be involved. In contrast, the rectangle shapes only represent tasks that are fulfilled automatically without human interaction.

The initial task that concerns both Service and Test Development is the definition of a "Service Description". This is a document that can be understood as a requirements specification and is created by the service provider in consultation with a customer. It contains all possible demands a customer might have for a specific value added service. To simplify the creation process of the "Service Description", the service provider provides the customer with a so-called "Requirements Catalogue". This catalogue contains predefined standards, restrictions and requirements. The selection of these predefined aspects for a specific value added service results in a form of service description. Furthermore, the relevant roles for the usage of a service are identified within this document.

After the "Service Description" is defined, both the "Service Development" and the "Test Development" are triggered in parallel. The "Service Development" part already exists in the TeamCom Service Creation Environment (Eichelmann et al., 2008). The service creation within TeamCom works as follows: a service designer describes the business process of the corresponding value added service through a formal control logic based on BPEL. So that the modelling of the business process can be done correctly, it requires the usage of predefined communication building blocks which cover the functionality of typical service aspects. This concept of using elementary communication service components is a key advantage of the approach because it hides the underlying heterogeneous communication networks. Thus, the service designer does not need any detailed knowledge of certain communication protocols and is able to focus on the application logic instead. As BPEL has not been developed for control of real time communication services in heterogeneous networks, a code generator respectively "Service Generator" has been implemented to translate the business process description into Java code. The generated code is based on the JAIN SLEE (Sun and Open Cloud, 2008) architecture, as this technology fulfils the necessity of communication services. The final step of the approach is the deployment of the code on a specific JAIN SLEE Application Server such as Mobicents (Mobicents, 2010).

In parallel with the "Service Development" process, the "Test Development" process is initiated by a test developer. First of all, the test developer has to interpret the "Service Description" properly and also has to extract the relevant service information for the test purpose. Afterwards, he has to choose the service related characteristics out of a repository of predefined modular finite state machines. These state machines cover typical service characteristics like protocol sequences for TCP (Transmission Control Protocol), SIP (Session Initiation Protocol) or HTTP (Hypertext Transfer Protocol). By composing the chosen predefined modular finite state machines, the test developer creates a behaviour model, which describes the possible behaviour of a value added service. Depending on the service's complexity, the behaviour model itself is also a more or less complex finite state machine. If the behaviour model is complete, an algorithm generates the service specific test cases by identifying every possible path through the finite state machine. A behaviour model can be seen as complete, if all the requirements specified in the "Service Description" are covered within the model.

After the generation is done, every identified test case is converted to TTCN-3 (Testing and Test Control Notation Version 3) (TTCN-3, 2010) within the "Test Case Generation" process. TTCN-3 is an abstract test scripting language which was standardized by ETSI (ETSI, 2010) and ITU-T (ITU-T, 2010) and supports the modularized creation of test scenarios for message and procedure based systems. In the ComGeneration approach, the execution of the generated TTCN-3 test cases on the deployed service is done within a TTCN-3 test framework.

3. Service Description

Defining the "Service Description" for a specific value added service is maybe the most important aspect within the process of creating a service, because it can be seen as a kind of contract between a customer and a service provider. It enables the customer to communicate his requirements for a service to the service developer so that the service can be realized properly. For the ComGeneration project, a specific way of defining a "Service Description" has been developed. It has been derived from a standardized object oriented method and includes the following steps:

1. Short description
2. Identification of the roles (without the system)
3. Requirements specification (with customer)
4. Enhanced requirements specification (without customer)
5. Identification of the communication interfaces

The initial step is to write a very short description about the service's functionality. Exemplarily, this is shown for the Web2IM (Web-to-Instant-Message) service:

A website should deliver two input masks. The first input mask should contain the address or telephone number (SIP URI) of any participant and the second one should carry any kind of text. A button should be integrated on the web site. When submitting it, the text included in the second input mask should be transferred to the address that was filled in the first input mask. If the SIP URI is not reachable or the text couldn't be transferred an error should occur on the web site. If the transfer worked, a success message should occur.

This short description of the service is followed by the second step, the identification of the roles respectively participants. For the Web2IM example, this would be on the one hand a web browser ([B]) and on the other hand a text display unit. As SIP is used to transfer the text, the display unit could be a SIP softphone ([S]).

The third step to define a "Service Description" requires the cooperation of the customer and the service developer. Both define significant cases that may occur when using the service. The table illustrates a possible case for the Web2IM service.

			Role
Preconditions	Website available		[B]
	SIP URI entered		[B]
	Text entered		[B]
	Entry approved		[B]
Target	Softphone reachable		[S]
Postcondition	Softphone gets text		[S]
	Approval is displayed		[B]
Description	After accessing the website, SIP URI and text are entered. Entries are approved and text is delivered to the softphone with the SIP URI. The receipt is approved on the website.		

Table 1: Standard case for requirements specification of Web2IM service

Depending on the kind of service, a few of such cases may have to be identified. Afterwards, some enhanced requirements are defined without the customer in step 4 of the "Service Description" process. Here, some specific information is defined such as the maximal length of the SIP URI or the input text.

In the last step, the communication interfaces for the service are identified. This is very helpful information for the test developer, because he will then be able to choose the relevant modular finite state machines from the repository to build a behaviour model. For the Web2IM service, the communication interfaces are the following two: HTTP Client and SIP UAC nonInvite.

4. Test Development

The most significant aspect of this paper is the generation and execution process of test cases for specific value added services to verify that they meet the demands of the customer's requirements. For this purpose, Figure 2 shows the relevant steps for "Test Development" in detail.

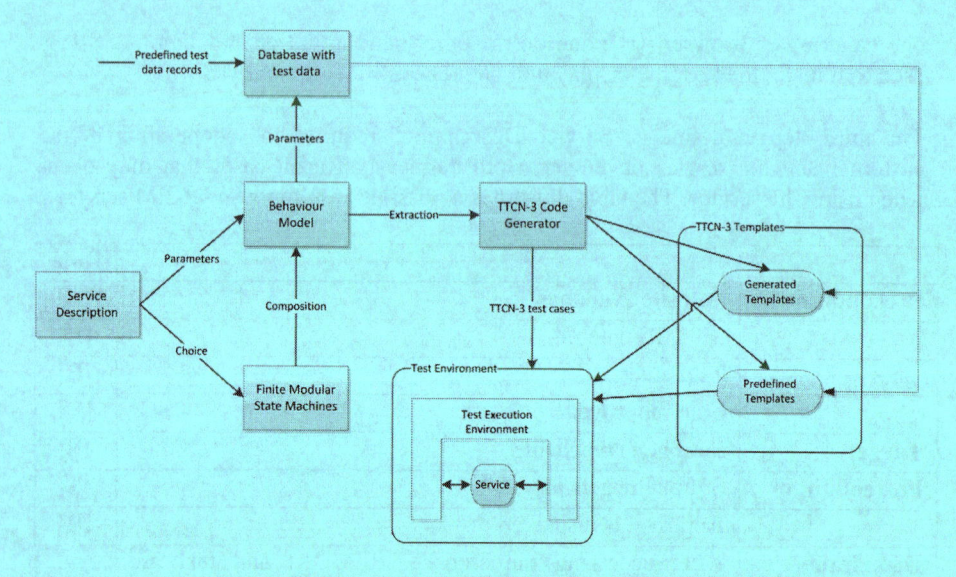

Figure 2: Test Development process

As already shown in Figure 1 and now also in Figure 2, the first condition to start the process is an existing "Service Description". On the basis of the description, the relevant finite modular state machines are chosen and composed to a behaviour model. It was already mentioned in the previous section that some important service related parameters can be specified within the "Service Description" that also have to be integrated into the behaviour model. In TTCN-3, parameters and their values are defined as TTCN-3 templates. This leads to the fact that every parameter within the behaviour model has to be transformed to a TTCN-3 template. An example for a relevant parameter within the behaviour model could be the name of a SIP instant message (e.g. "MESSAGE"). This could mean that during the service flow such a message is expected to be sent, e.g. to a specific SIP User Agent. The information of possible message structures used within the behaviour model has to be available during the "Test Development" process. So, a database with test data is required. In this database, many possible test data records are predefined as TTCN-3 templates. These templates can be enhanced by the data from the behaviour model. One has to distinguish between predefined and generated templates. Predefined templates already exist in the database, even before the behaviour model was created. Depending on which finite modular state machines are used within the model, the predefined templates are activated and integrated within the test framework. The generated templates are completely new. They are associated to the parameter inputs made by the test developer.

The last step of the "Test Development" process is the testing of the service itself within the test framework. This can only be done if all the extracted test cases exist as TTCN-3 test cases and all the relevant TTCN-3 templates were activated respectively generated and integrated into the test environment.

4.1. Modular finite state machines

Before the structure of the behaviour model is introduced, first the components, the modular finite state machines, are described. The finite state machines are predefined and reusable components which are usually based on specific protocols (SIP, TCP, HTTP) or categories (databases). The structure of the finite state machines for the protocols is derived from the particular protocol specification. Depending on the specification, each finite state machine can have several inputs and outputs. These interfaces are used to compose more finite state machines with each other and to enable the building of the behaviour model.

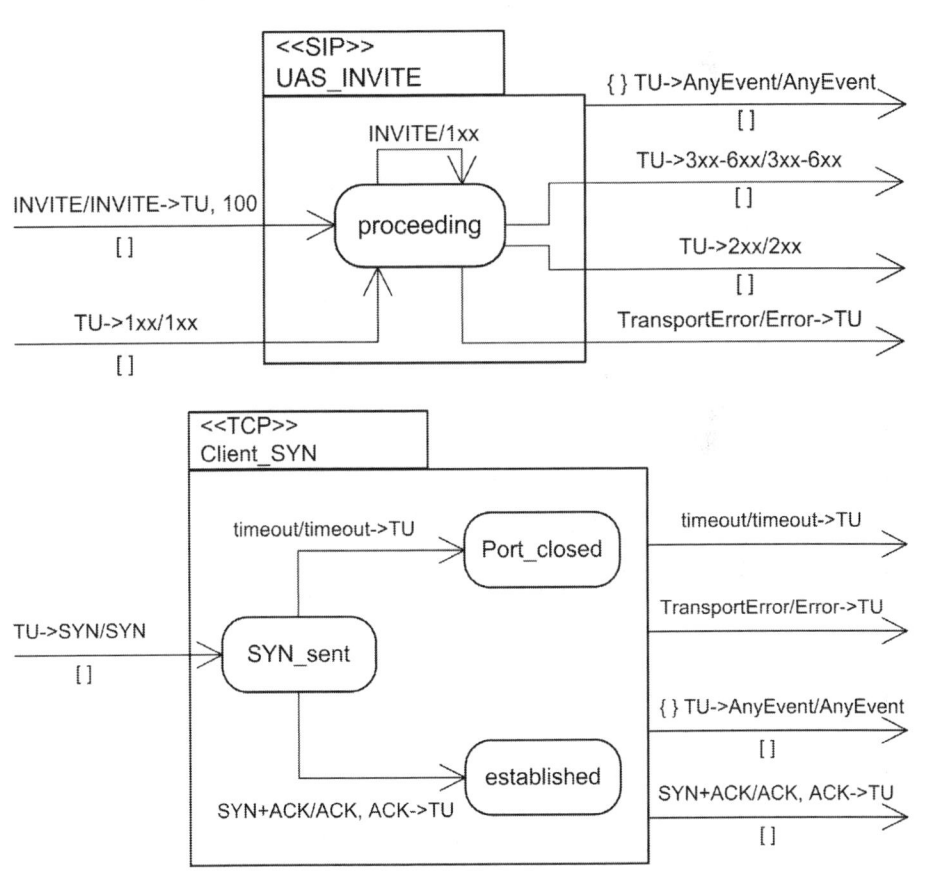

Figure 3: Structure of the finite state machines SIP UAS_Invite and TCP Client_SYN

Figure 3 shows exemplarily the structure of the finite state machines with the help of the two components SIP UAS_INVITE and TCP Client_SYN.

The finite state machine SIP UAS_INVITE describes the handling of an incoming SIP INVITE message for a User Agent Server (UAS). Every incoming and outgoing transition represents a message that either is received or sent by the UAS. The possible responses, which can be initiated by the User Agent Server, are defined as outputs. Besides the relevant protocol specific outputs like the SIP status codes (2xx, 3xx-6xx) and occurring transport errors, there is also a so-called "AnyEvent" defined. This output can be understood as a placeholder for any kind of message from any protocol. This technique enables the composing of all available finite state machines.

The structure of the finite state machine TCP Client_SYN is a little bit different from the SIP UAS_INVITE, as there are three existent states within the finite state machine. The internal transitions between these states are fixed and always used in the same manner. The TCP Client_SYN represents a TCP connection establishment. The meaning of the "TU" statement within the transitions is discussed in the following section 4.2.

A test developer only knows about the available finite state machines from specific protocols. His main task to build a behaviour model is to handle the interfaces of the finite state machines.

4.2. Behaviour model

In order to do functional testing of a value added service, a test developer has to know, how the service should behave according to the specification, if, for instance, certain messages occur. This knowledge can be retrieved from the "Service Description". If the understanding of the service is fulfilled, the test developer chooses the relevant modular finite state machines and composes them to get the behaviour model. The composition of finite state machines is the only changing component, the internal transitions, however, are unchangeable. In order to assure, that a behaviour model can be established, a new concept, the Transaction User (TU), was installed. The TU perceives itself as a switching unit between the possible roles of an Application Server (AS) as User Agent Server and User Agent Client. Concurrently, the TU is a connector between modular finite state machines. It enables the test developer to reproduce the service logic for test purposes.

An example of composing the finite state machines from different protocols (Figure 3) is shown in Figure 4. This service logic could be interpreted as follows: the service expects calls from a selection of User Agents (alice, bob). Only if these User Agents call the service, a TCP connection to a specific socket (IP, Port), e.g. to an external database, is established. Here, the SIP INVITE is a sort of trigger.

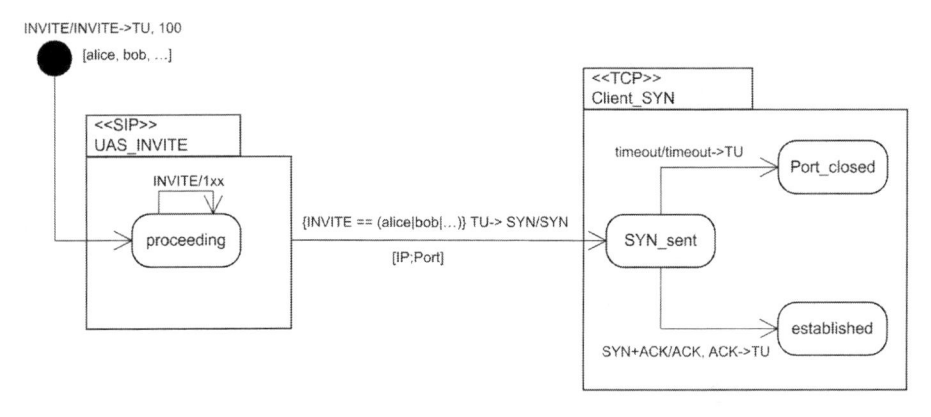

Figure 4: Exemplary role of the TU as a connector of finite state machines

The composition of the two finite state machines is done by using the input message from the TCP Client_SYN as the AnyEvent output message of the SIP UAS_INVITE. Figure 5 clarifies the whole concept of the TU.

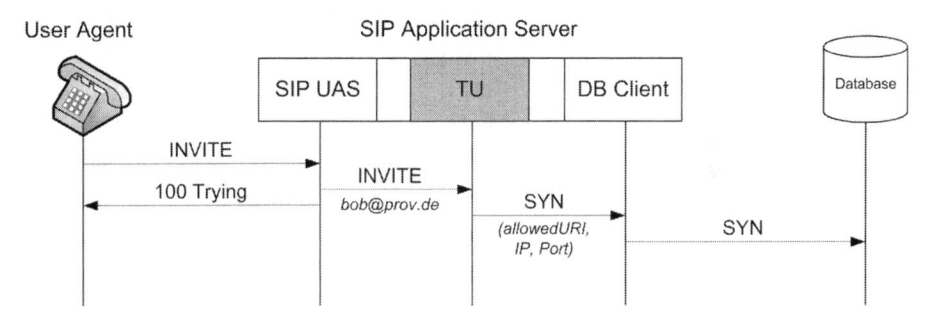

Figure 5: Equivalent message flow by traversing the behaviour model

The demonstrated message flow in Figure 5 reflects the transition path within the finite state machine shown in Figure 4.

When the test developer creates a behaviour model for a value added service he does not need to have any information about the insides of a finite state machine, because he only has to handle the interfaces and has to set relevant parameters. Figure 6 demonstrates a simplified but complete behaviour model of the Web2IM service which was introduced in section 3. The two HTTP modular finite state machines, Server_Req and Server_Resp, represent the initiation of the POST request and the expected responses from the server. In contrast, the three SIP modular finite state machines describe the behaviour of the SIP Message being sent by the service. As the service is the sender of the SIP Message, only the UAC finite state machines are considered.

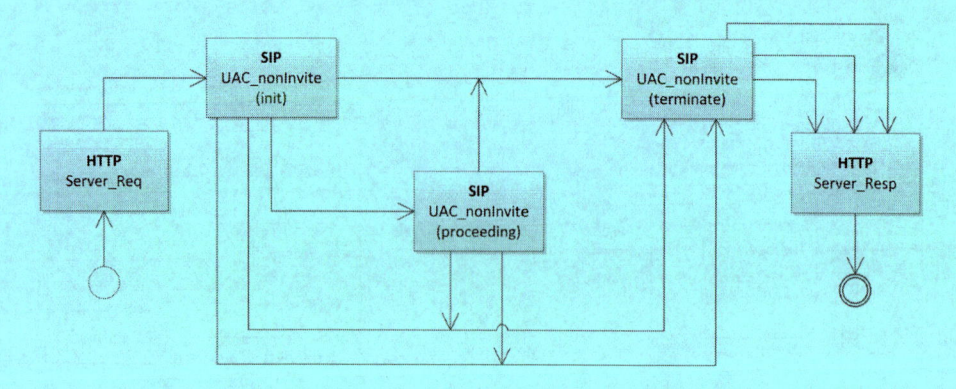

Figure 6: Behaviour model for the value added service Web2IM

4.3. Test Case Generation

The main argument for using finite state machines as behaviour models is that the transition paths within a state machine represent test cases for a value added service. Therefore, an algorithm has to be defined that identifies all the possible paths. Such an algorithm has not yet been realized as the implementation phase of the ComGeneration project has started recently.

The path finding within the behaviour model can be associated to the following criteria:

- state coverage: every state has to be visited once

- transition coverage: every transition has to be passed once

- event coverage: every possible event has to occur once

For every above-mentioned criterion, the identification of paths respectively the generation of test cases is fulfilled. Afterwards, when the test cases are available, they are transferred to real TTCN-3 test cases by a TTCN-3 code generator.

5. Test Execution

After the generation of the TTCN-3 test cases for a specific value added service has been done, the test cases have to be executed on the service respectively the System under Test (SUT). For this purpose, a TTCN-3 test execution environment is required. Within the ComGeneration project, the integrated test development and execution environment TTworkbench is used, which was developed by Testing Technologies (Testing Technologies, 2010). In order to connect the test execution environment to the SUT, a system adapter is required. Such a system adapter contains adapters that are relevant to enable the communication with the SUT.

Using the example of the Web2IM service, which has been introduced in the previous section, the system adapter would possibly contain a UDP adapter and a HTTP adapter. The UDP adapter is responsible for transferring SIP messages and it is configured to map the TTCN-3 ports to the UDP ports. As in TTCN-3 messages are defined as data structures, the test case executives will use the SIP codec for encoding the data structures to real SIP text messages and vice versa. For the usage of HTTP requests and responses that are used to trigger the service, there is also an adapter required.

Before the test cases can be executed, PTCs (Parallel Test Component) have to be configured that represent the relevant endpoints. For the Web2IM service, two different PTCs have to be defined. The first PTC sends the initial HTTP request to the SUT which contains the text message and the SIP URI and receives the HTTP response with the failure or success message. In contrast, the second PTC receives the SIP MESSAGE from the SUT and answers with a specific SIP status code.

Figure 7 illustrates the structure of the TTCN-3 testing environment for the Web2IM service.

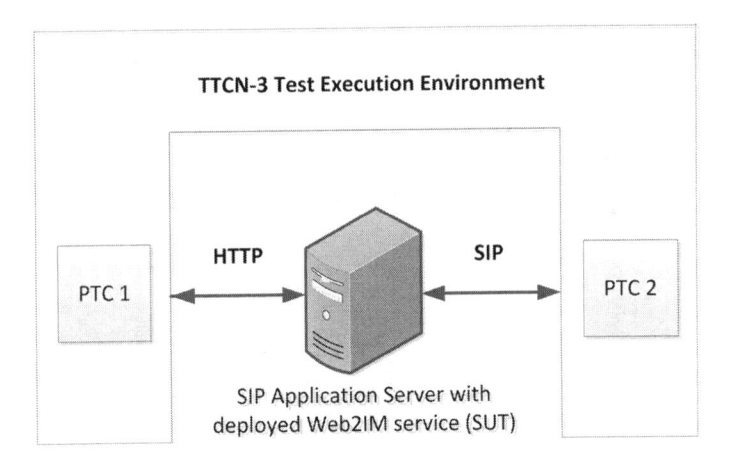

Figure 7: Test Execution Environment for Web2IM service

6. Conclusion

In this paper, we have introduced an approach to integrate functional testing within an existing SCE to validate that a created value added service meets the requirements of the customer who ordered the service. For the testing purpose, a test developer has to get a deep knowledge about the service requirements from the "Service Description" and then has to build an abstract model in the form of a finite state machine, the behaviour model. Although the creation of such a behaviour model tends to be complicated, the advantages dominate, because the extraction of test cases from the model can be done easily with an adequate algorithm.

Once the behaviour model has been developed, it takes very little time until the execution of the generated test cases on the SUT can be done. With the support of quite a lot of communication protocols like SIP, TCP or HTTP, many sorts of value added services can be tested. Besides these positive effects of such an implementation, the test developer who uses the tool has to have a deep knowledge of every used protocol.

As soon as the ComGeneration development environment is implemented, which enables the creation of a behaviour model, an evaluation of the approach is required. To prove the reduction of time and costs in comparison with manual testing, both procedures have to be accomplished for a couple of exemplary value added services.

7. Acknowledgment

The research project ComGeneration providing the basis for this publication was partially funded by the Federal Ministry of Education and Research (BMBF) of the Federal Republic of Germany under grand number 1724B09. The authors of this publication are in charge of its content.

8. References

ComGeneration Project Web Site (2010): http://www.ecs.fh-osnabrueck.de/27619.html. (Accessed 15 August 2010)

Conformiq (2010): http://www.conformiq.com . (Accessed 20 August 2010)

Eichelmann, T., Fuhrmann, W., Trick, U. and Ghita, B. (2008), "Creation of value added services in NGN with BPEL", *SEIN*, Wrexham, 2008

ETSI Testing and Test Control Notation (TTCN-3) (2010): http://www.etsi.org/WebSite/technologies/ttcn3.aspx. (Accessed 14 August 2010)

ITU-T – The Evolution of TTCN (2010): http://www.itu.int/ITU-T/studygroups/com07/ttcn.html (Accessed 14 August 2010)

Lehmann, A., Eichelmann, T., Trick, U., Lasch, R., Ricks, B. and Tönjes, R. (2009), "TeamCom: A Service Creation Environment for Next Generation Networks", ICIW, Venice, 2009

Mobicents Open Source JAIN SLEE Server Project Web Site (2010): http://www.mobicents.org. (Accessed 14 August 2010)

Sun Microsystems, Open Cloud (2008), JSR-000240 Specification, Final Release, "JAIN SLEE (JSLEE) 1.1", Sun.

TeamCom Project Web Site (2009): http://www.ecs.fh-osnabrueck.de/teamcom.html. (Accessed 14 August 2010)

TTMedal (2010): http://www.tt-medal.org, (Accessed 20 August 2010)

Testing Technologies (2010): http://www.testingtech.com. (Accessed 15 August 2010)

TTCN-3 application areas (2010): http://www.ttcn-3.org/ApplicationAreas.htm. (Accessed 14 August 2010)

Author Index

Atkinson, S 1, 43

Bleimann, U 1
Buchheit, M 43

Dowland, PS 19, 53

Eichelmann, T 61

Fischer-Hellmann, KP 1
Fuhrmann, W 11, 61
Furnell, SM 31, 43

George, M 1
Ghita, BV 11, 61
Glaab, M 11

Harriehausen, B 31

Knahl, M 1, 43
Knirsch, A 19
Knoll, M 31
Krey, M 31

Lehmann, A 61

Mairon, K 43
Moore, R 19

Schreier, U 43
Schütte, A 53

Trick, U 61

Vergata, S 53

Wacht, P 61
Wietzke, J 11, 19, 53